ATAR GULL

OR THE TALE OF A MODEL SLAVE

Based on the novel by Eugène Sue

Writer: Fabien Nury
Artist: Brüno
Colorist: Laurence Croix

ALSO FROM
FABIEN NURY.

THE DEATH OF STALIN
DEATH TO THE TSAR
TYLER CROSS:BLACK ROCK
TYER CROSS:ANGOLA

THE CHRONICLES OF LEGION - BOOK 1:
RISE OF THE VAMPIRES

THE CHRONICLES OF LEGION - BOOK 2:
THE THREE LIVES OF DRACULA

THE CHRONICLES OF LEGION - BOOK 3:
THE BLOOD BROTHERS

THE CHRONICLES OF LEGION - BOOK 4:
THE THREE FACES OF EVIL

ALSO FROM TITAN COMICS AND
STATIX PRESS

2021: LOST CHILDREN

ALISIK: FALL

ATLAS & AXIS

THE BEAUTIFUL DEATH

CENTURY'S END

THE CHIMERA BRIGADE - BOOK 1

THE CHIMERA BRIGADE - BOOK 2

THE CHIMERA BRIGADE - BOOK 3

THE CHRONICLES OF LEGION - BOOK 1:RISE OF THE VAMPIRES

THE CHRONICLES OF LEGION - BOOK 2: THE THREE LIVES OF DRACULA

DEAD LIFE

DOCTOR RADAR

EMMA G. WILDFORD

EXTERMINATOR 17

FACTORY

HERCULES: WRATH OF THE HEAVENS

KHAAL

KONUNGAR: WAR OF CROWNS

THE 6 VOYAGES OF LONE SLOANE

LONE SLOANE: DELIRIUS

LONE SLOANE: GAIL

LONE SLOANE: SALAMMBÔ

MANCHETTE'S FATALE

MASKED: RISE OF THE ROCKET

MCCAY

MONIKA - BOOK 1: MASKED BALL

MONIKA - BOOK 2: VANILLA DOLLS

MONSTER

THE NIKOPOL TRILOGY

NORMAN - VOLUME 1

NORMAN - VOLUME 2: TEACHER'S PET

NORMAN - VOLUME 3: THE VENGEANCE OF GRACE

NORMAN: THE FIRST SLASH

OSCAR MARTIN'S SOLO: THE SURVIVORS OF CHAOS

PACIFIC

THE QUEST FOR THE TIME BIRD

THE RAGE - BOOK 1: ZOMBIE GENERATION

THE RAGE - BOOK 2: KILL OR CURE

RAVINA THE WITCH?

ROYAL BLOOD

SAMURAI: THE ISLE WITH NO NAME

SAMURAI: BROTHERS IN ARMS

THE SEASON OF THE SNAKE

SHERLOCK FOX

SHOWMAN KILLER - BOOK 1: HEARTLESS HERO

SHOWMAN KILLER - BOOK 2: THE GOLDEN CHILD

SHOWMAN KILLER - BOOK 3: THE INVISIBLE WOMAN

SKY DOLL: SPACESHIP

SKY DOLL: DECADE

SKY DOLL: SUDRA

SNOWPIERCER: THE ESCAPE

SNOWPIERCER: THE EXPLORERS

SNOWPIERCER: TERMINUS

THE THIRD TESTAMENT - BOOK 1: THE LION AWAKES

THE THIRD TESTAMENT - BOOK 2: THE ANGEL'S FACE

THE THIRD TESTAMENT - BOOK 3: THE MIGHT OF THE OX

THE THIRD TESTAMENT - BOOK 4: THE DAY OF THE RAVEN

UNDER: SCOURGE OF THE SEWER

UNIVERSAL WAR ONE

VOID

WORLD WAR X

YRAGAËL / URM THE MAD

Translated By Diane Eberhardt • Editor Jake Devine

TITAN COMICS

Managing Editor Martin Eden • Senior Creative Editor David Leach • Art Director Oz Browne • Senior Production Controller Jackie Flook • Production Controller Peter James • Production Assistant Rhiannon Roy • Sales & Circulation Manager Steve Tothill • Senior Publicist Will O'Mullane • Senior Brand Manager Chris Thompson • Publicist Imogen Harris • Ads & Marketing Assistant Bella Hoy • Commercial Manager Michelle Fairlamb • Publishing Director Darryl Tothill • Operations Director Leigh Baulch • Executive Director Vivian Cheung • Publisher Nick Landau

Atar Gull

9781785867323

Published by Titan Comics
A division of Titan Publishing Group Ltd.144 Southwark St., London, SE1 0UP.Titan Comics is a registered trademark of Titan Publishing Group. Ltd.All rights reserved.

Originally published in French as Atar Gull © Dargaud 2015 - Fabien Nury & Brüno

A CIP catalogue record for this title is available from the British Library

10 9 8 7 6 5 4 3 2 1
First Published September 2019
Printed in China.
Titan Comics.

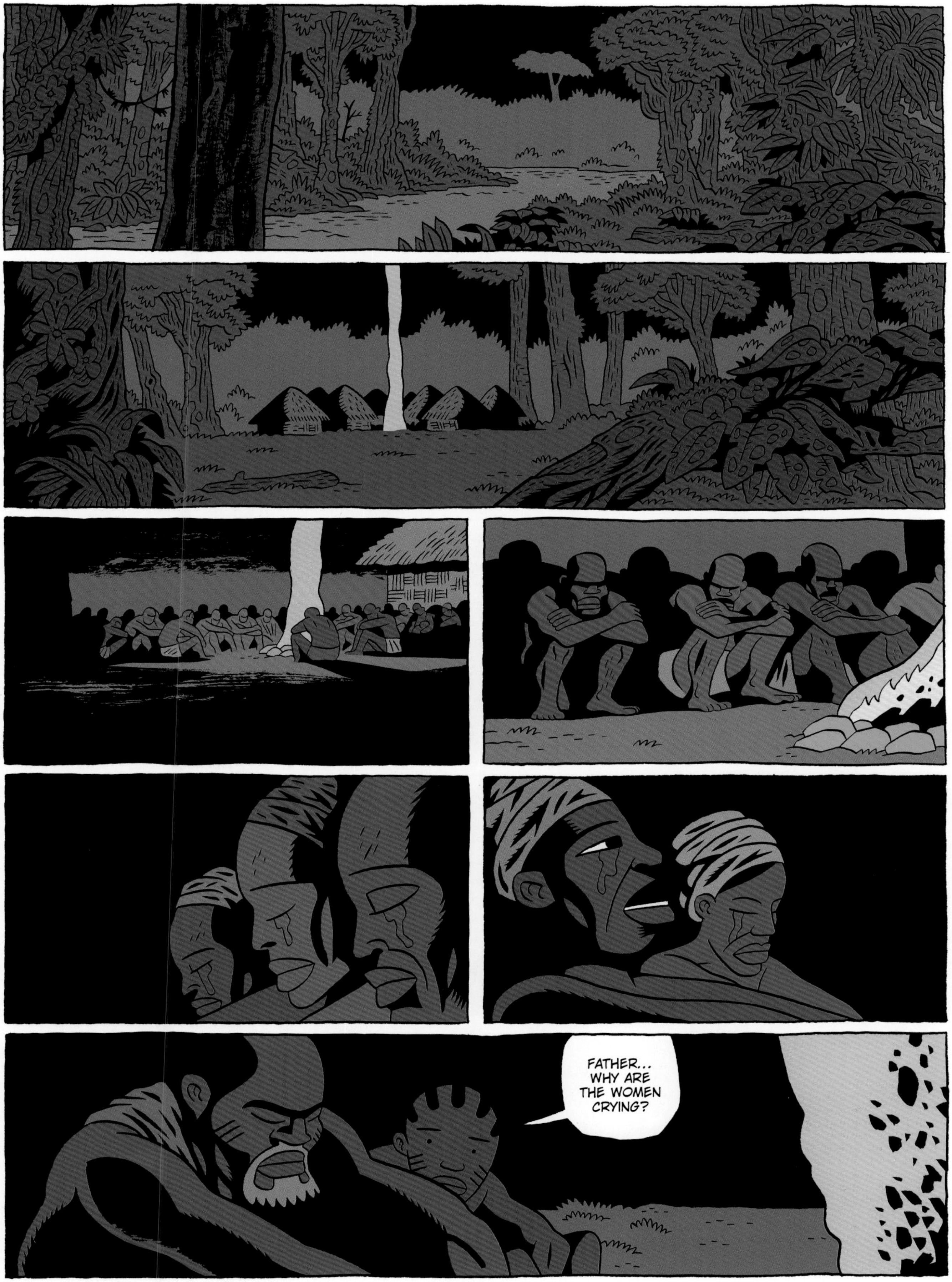
FATHER... WHY ARE THE WOMEN CRYING?

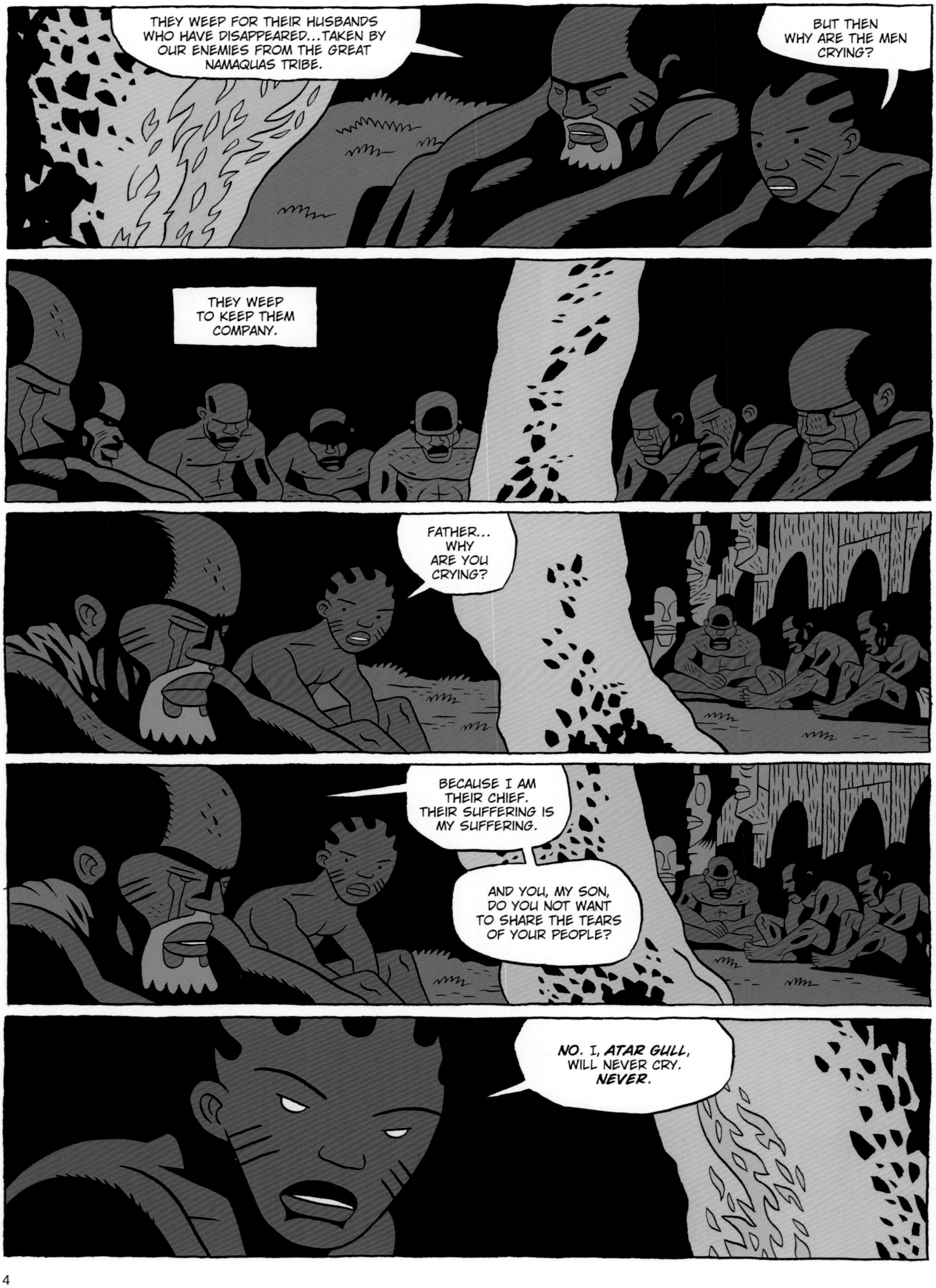
THEY WEEP FOR THEIR HUSBANDS WHO HAVE DISAPPEARED...TAKEN BY OUR ENEMIES FROM THE GREAT NAMAQUAS TRIBE.
BUT THEN WHY ARE THE MEN CRYING?
THEY WEEP TO KEEP THEM COMPANY.
FATHER... WHY ARE YOU CRYING?
BECAUSE I AM THEIR CHIEF. THEIR SUFFERING IS MY SUFFERING.
AND YOU, MY SON, DO YOU NOT WANT TO SHARE THE TEARS OF YOUR PEOPLE?
NO. I, ATAR GULL, WILL NEVER CRY. NEVER.

BOOK I

The Crossing

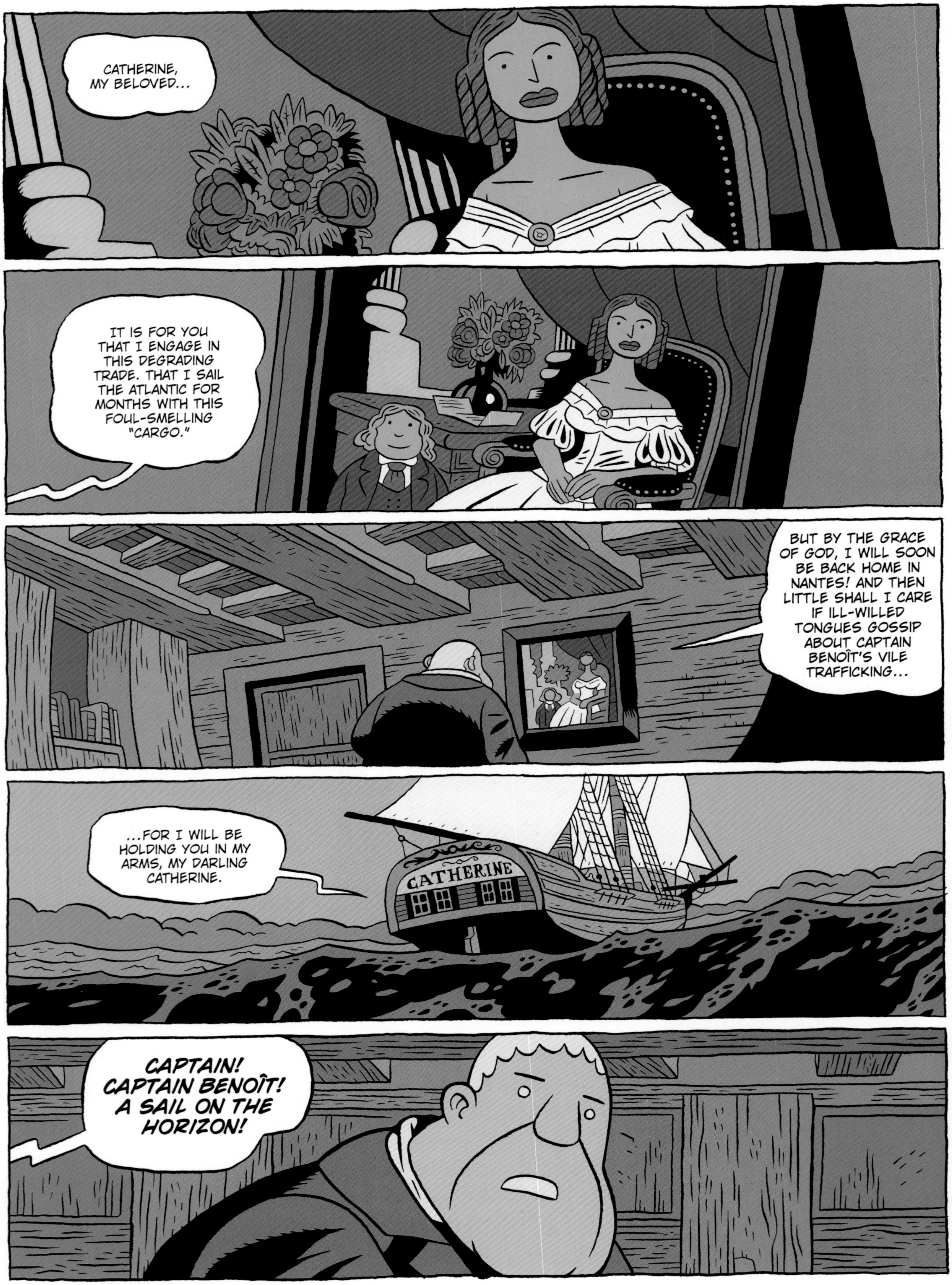
CATHERINE, MY BELOVED...
IT IS FOR YOU THAT I ENGAGE IN THIS DEGRADING TRADE. THAT I SAIL THE ATLANTIC FOR MONTHS WITH THIS FOUL-SMELLING "CARGO."
BUT BY THE GRACE OF GOD, I WILL SOON BE BACK HOME IN NANTES! AND THEN LITTLE SHALL I CARE IF ILL-WILLED TONGUES GOSSIP ABOUT CAPTAIN BENOÎT'S VILE TRAFFICKING...
...FOR I WILL BE HOLDING YOU IN MY ARMS, MY DARLING CATHERINE.
CATHERINE
CAPTAIN! CAPTAIN BENOÎT! A SAIL ON THE HORIZON!

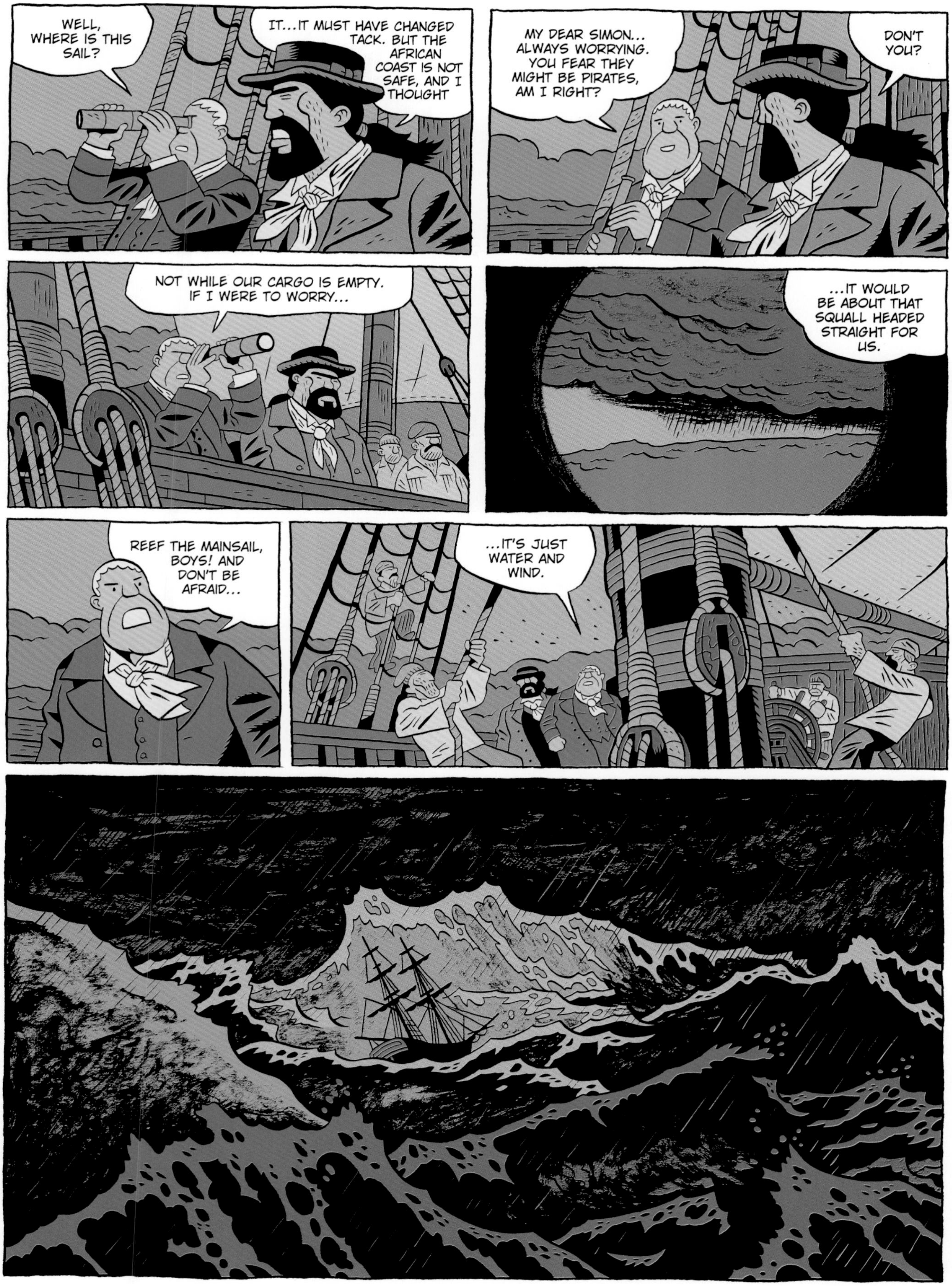
WELL, WHERE IS THIS SAIL?
IT...IT MUST HAVE CHANGED TACK. BUT THE AFRICAN COAST IS NOT SAFE, AND I THOUGHT
MY DEAR SIMON... ALWAYS WORRYING. YOU FEAR THEY MIGHT BE PIRATES, AM I RIGHT?
DON'T YOU?
NOT WHILE OUR CARGO IS EMPTY. IF I WERE TO WORRY...
...IT WOULD BE ABOUT THAT SQUALL HEADED STRAIGHT FOR US.
REEF THE MAINSAIL, BOYS! AND DON'T BE AFRAID...
...IT'S JUST WATER AND WIND.

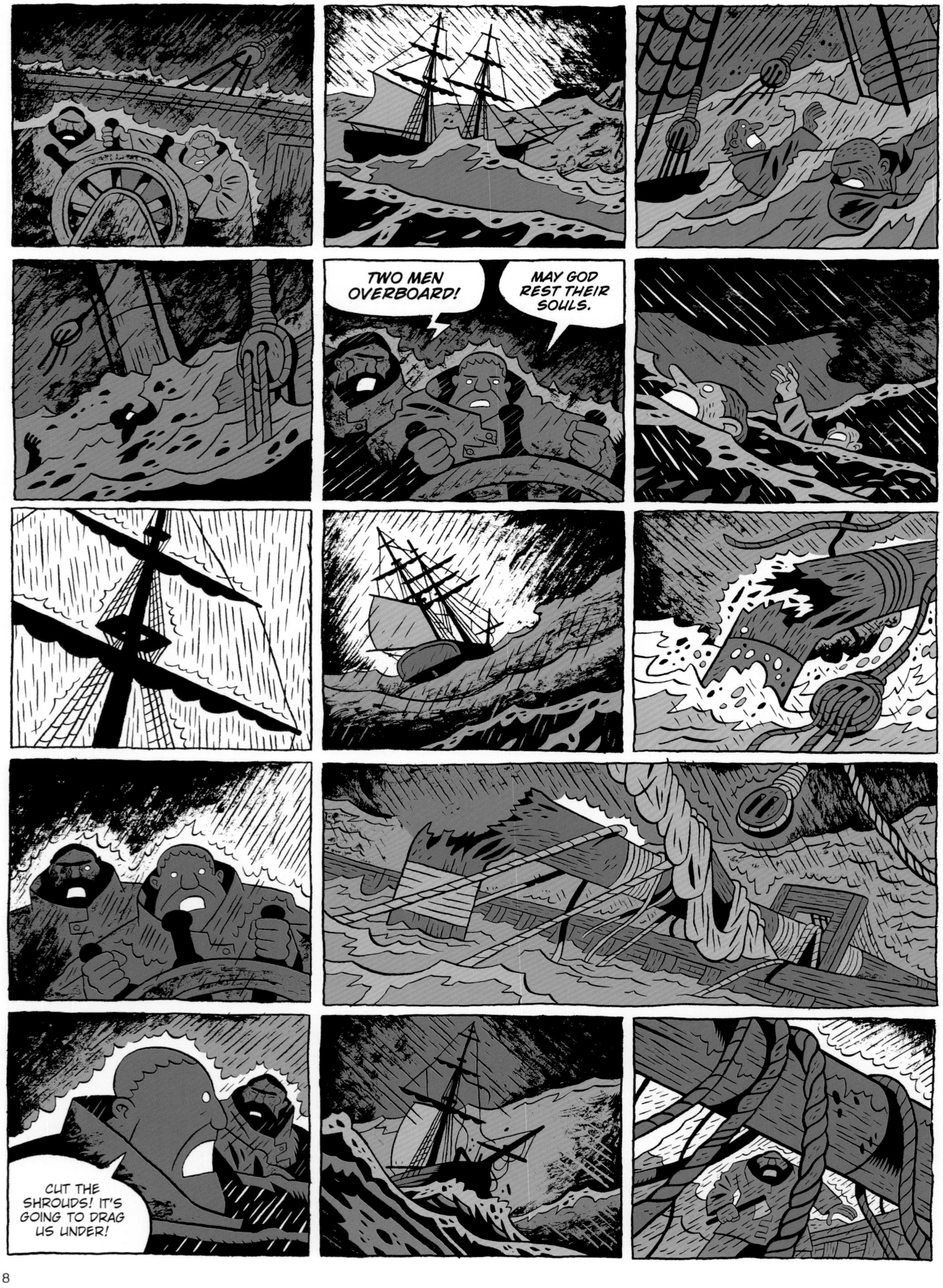
TWO MEN OVERBOARD!
MAY GOD REST THEIR SOULS.
CUT THE SHROUDS! IT'S GOING TO DRAG US UNDER!

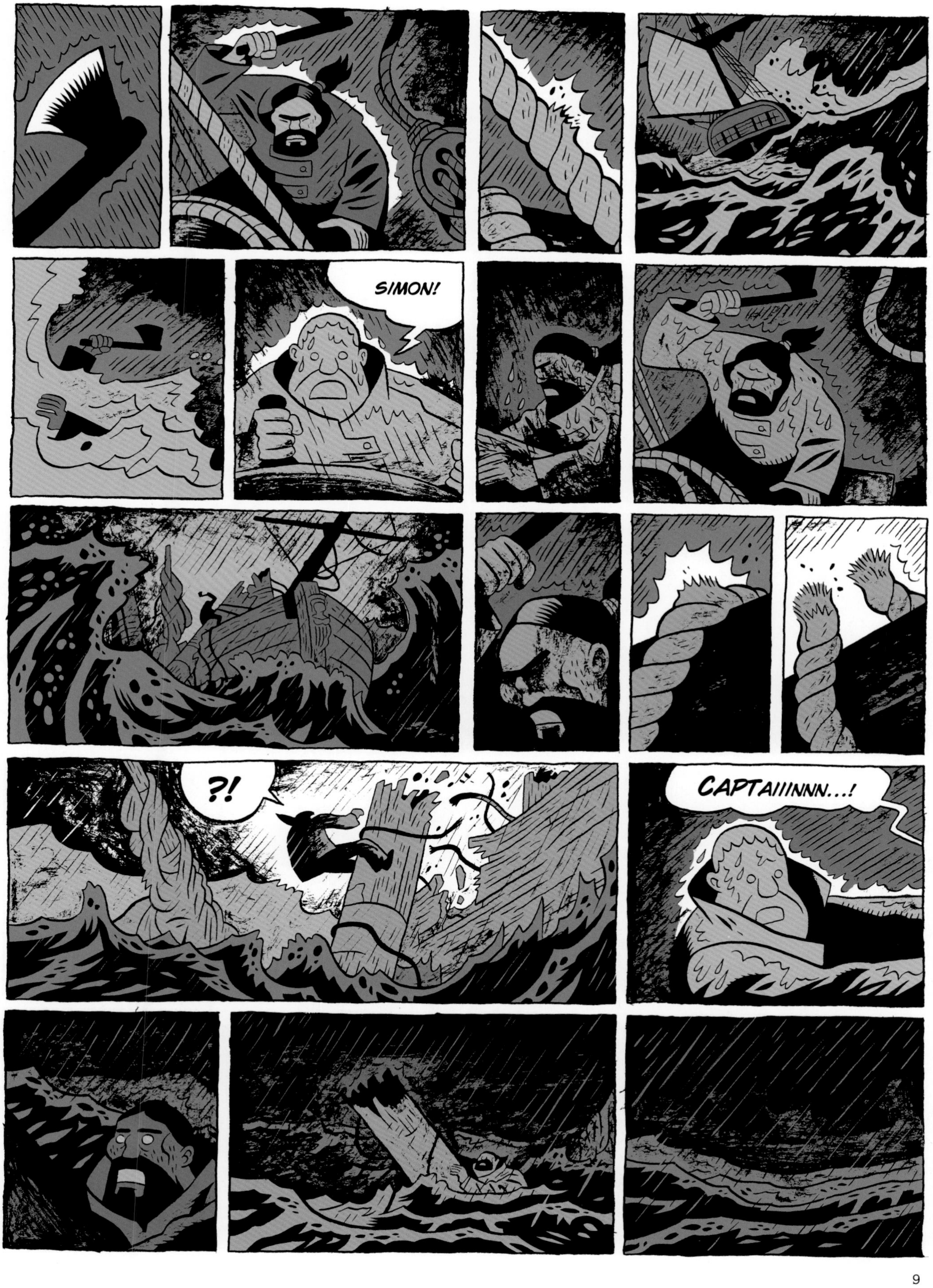
SIMON!
?!
CAPTAIIINNN...!

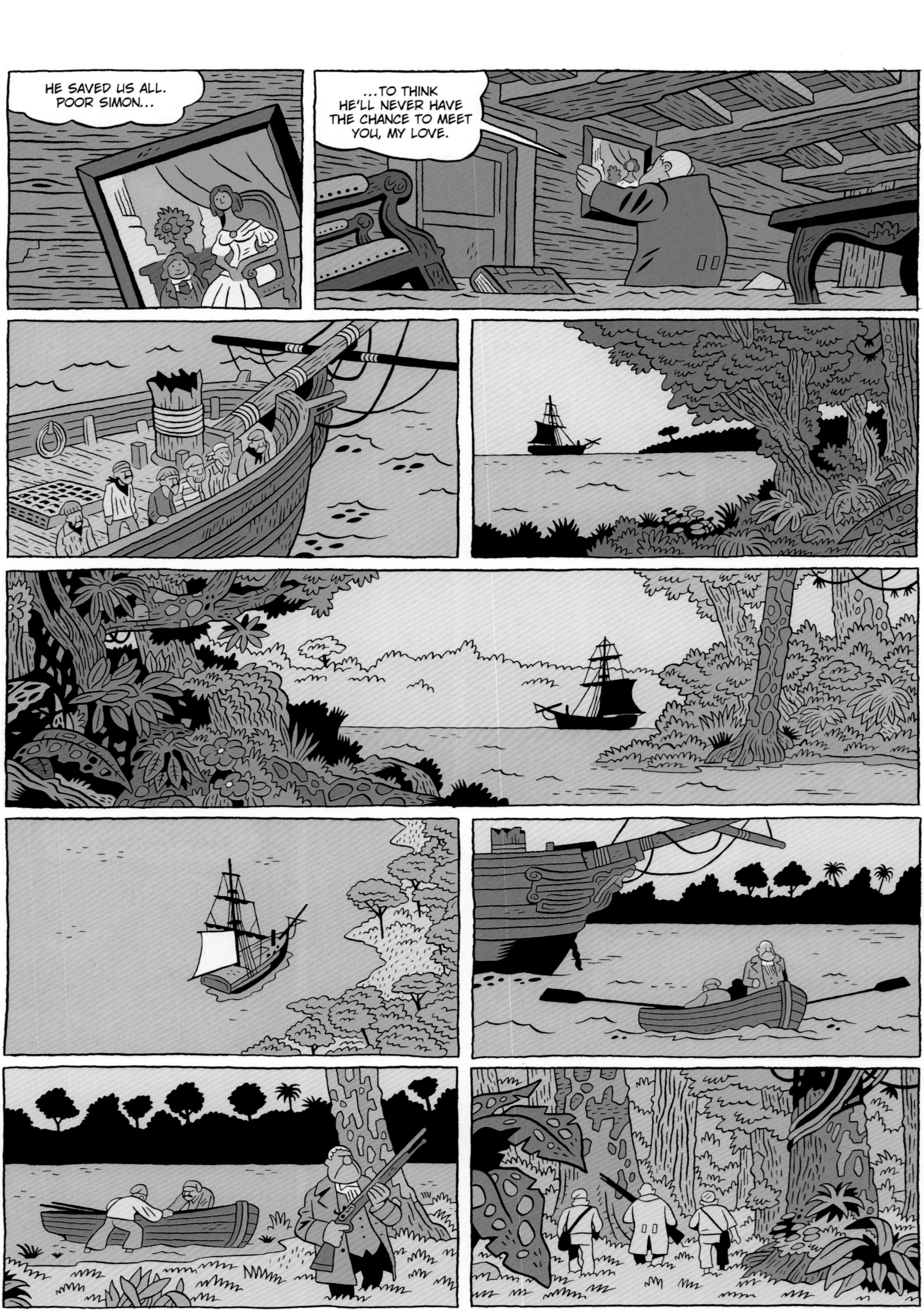
HE SAVED US ALL. POOR SIMON...
...TO THINK HE'LL NEVER HAVE THE CHANCE TO MEET YOU, MY LOVE.

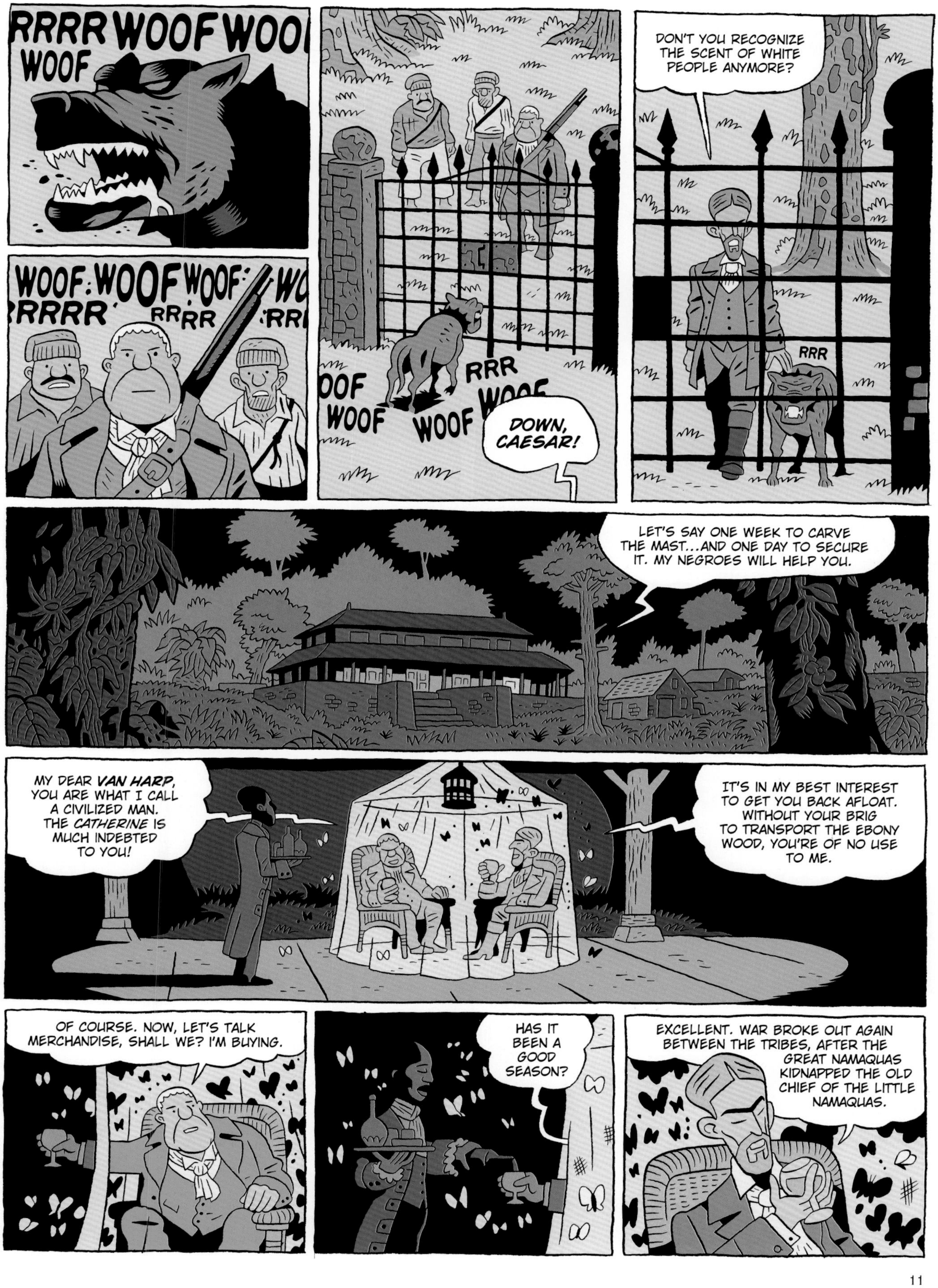
RRRR WOOF WOO
WOOF
WOOF WOOF WOOF WO
RRRRR RRRR RRR
OOF WOOF RRR WOOF WOOF
DOWN, CAESAR!
DON'T YOU RECOGNIZE THE SCENT OF WHITE PEOPLE ANYMORE?
RRR
LET'S SAY ONE WEEK TO CARVE THE MAST...AND ONE DAY TO SECURE IT. MY NEGROES WILL HELP YOU.
MY DEAR *VAN HARP*, YOU ARE WHAT I CALL A CIVILIZED MAN. THE *CATHERINE* IS MUCH INDEBTED TO YOU!
IT'S IN MY BEST INTEREST TO GET YOU BACK AFLOAT. WITHOUT YOUR BRIG TO TRANSPORT THE EBONY WOOD, YOU'RE OF NO USE TO ME.
OF COURSE. NOW, LET'S TALK MERCHANDISE, SHALL WE? I'M BUYING.
HAS IT BEEN A GOOD SEASON?
EXCELLENT. WAR BROKE OUT AGAIN BETWEEN THE TRIBES, AFTER THE GREAT NAMAQUAS KIDNAPPED THE OLD CHIEF OF THE LITTLE NAMAQUAS.

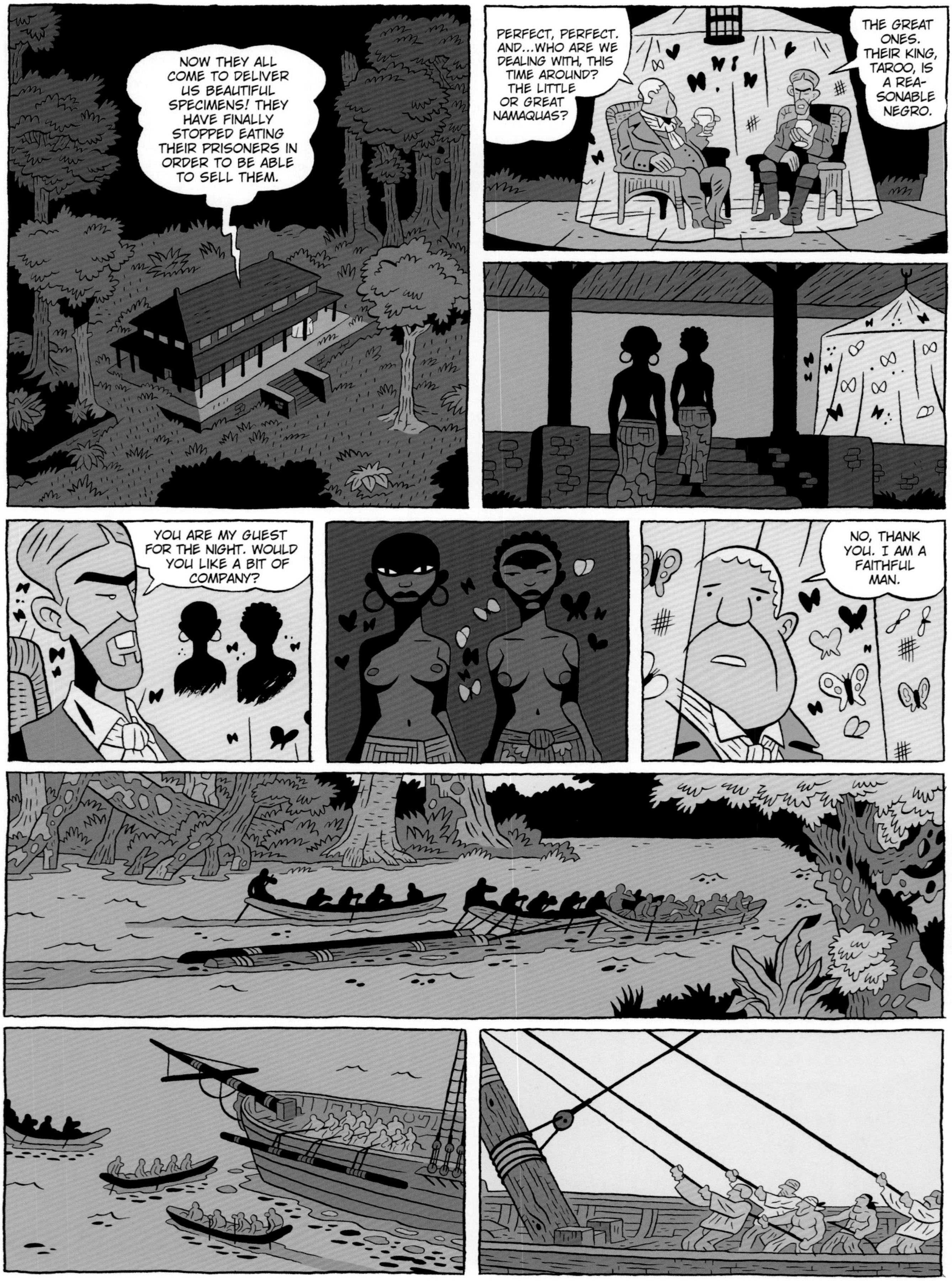
NOW THEY ALL COME TO DELIVER US BEAUTIFUL SPECIMENS! THEY HAVE FINALLY STOPPED EATING THEIR PRISONERS IN ORDER TO BE ABLE TO SELL THEM.
PERFECT, PERFECT. AND...WHO ARE WE DEALING WITH, THIS TIME AROUND? THE LITTLE OR GREAT NAMAQUAS?
THE GREAT ONES. THEIR KING, TAROO, IS A REASONABLE NEGRO.
YOU ARE MY GUEST FOR THE NIGHT. WOULD YOU LIKE A BIT OF COMPANY?
NO, THANK YOU. I AM A FAITHFUL MAN.

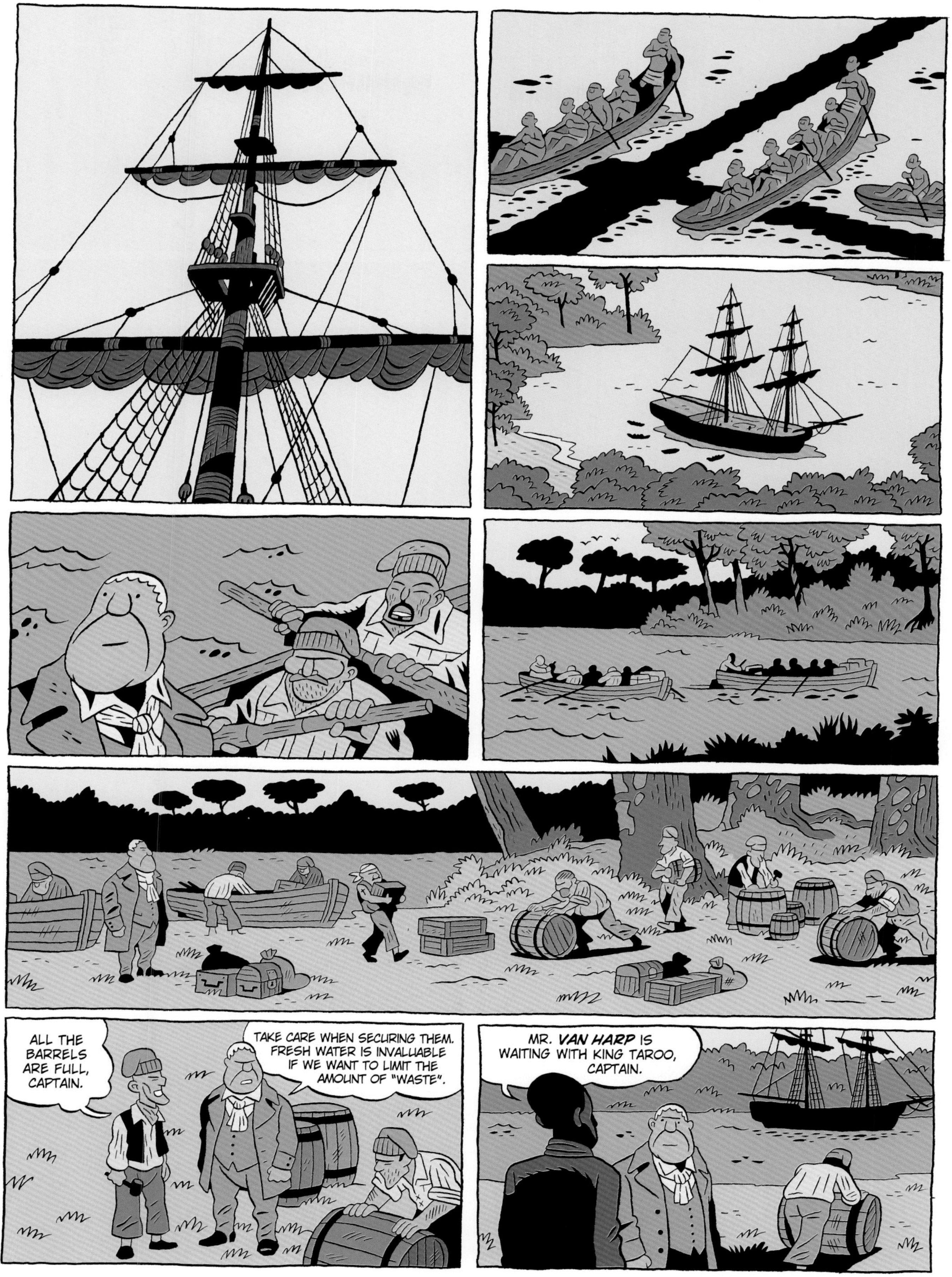
ALL THE BARRELS ARE FULL, CAPTAIN.
TAKE CARE WHEN SECURING THEM. FRESH WATER IS INVALUABLE IF WE WANT TO LIMIT THE AMOUNT OF "WASTE".
MR. VAN HARP IS WAITING WITH KING TAROO, CAPTAIN.

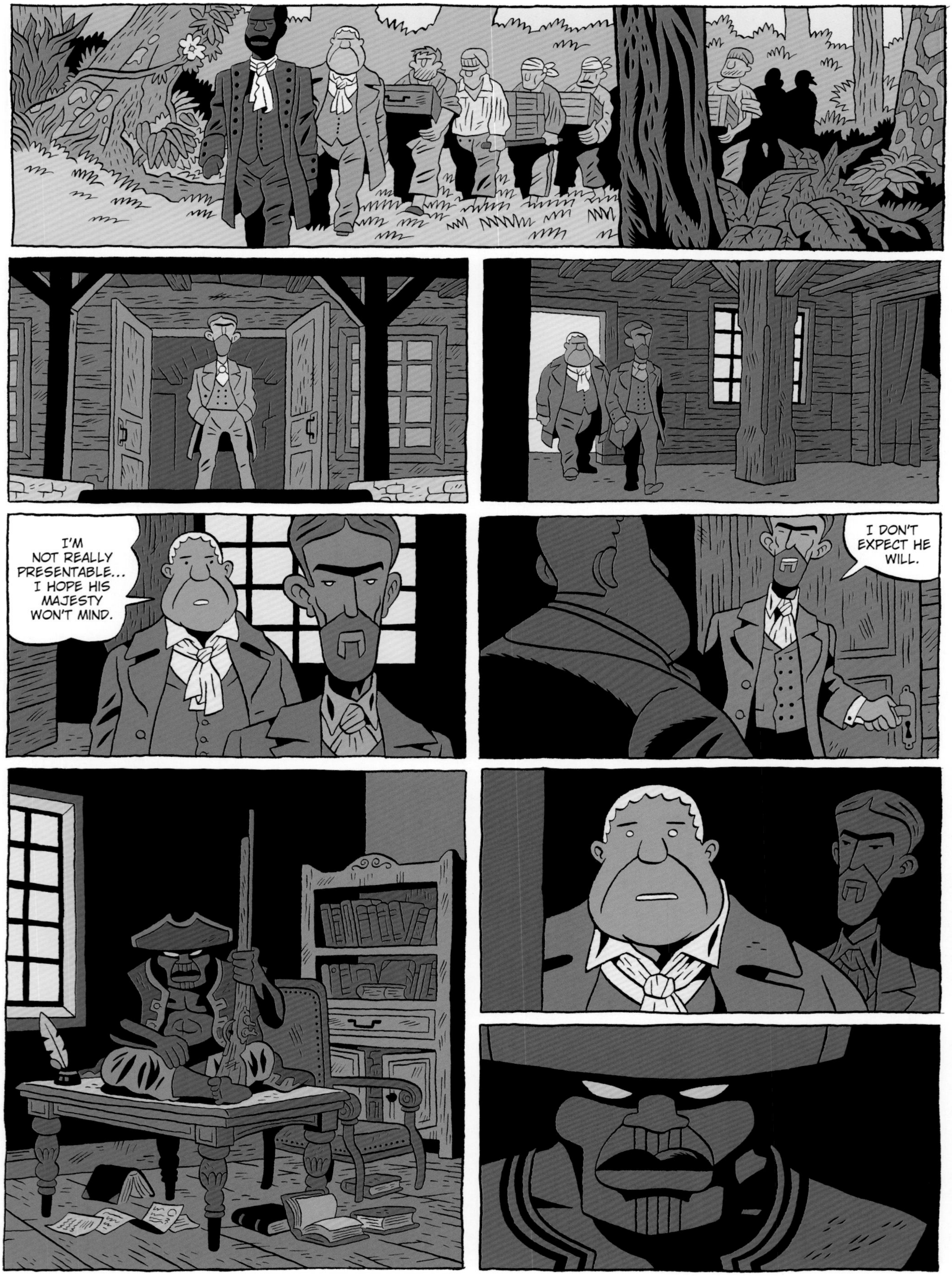
I'M NOT REALLY PRESENTABLE... I HOPE HIS MAJESTY WON'T MIND.
I DON'T EXPECT HE WILL.

I, Paul Van Harp, acting on behalf of Taroo, Chief of the tribe of the Great Namaquas, hereby sell, on behalf of the aforementioned Taroo, to Mr. Benoît (Claude, Bonomée, Martial), Captain of the brig named the Catherine:
32 negroes, of the Little Namaquas race, healthy, strong, and of solid physical stature, ages 20-30.
19 negresses of about the same age, two of which are pregnant and one with a newborn, which the seller is graciously offering below market price;
11 little negro boys and girls ages 9-12.
In total 32 negroes, 19 negresses, 11 negro children, which are delivered to Mr. Benoît in exchange for:
23 fully equipped rifles, with ramrods, batteries and bayonets,
5 quintals of gunpowder, 7 quintals of bar iron,
8 quintals of lead lingots,
And 6 cases of glass beads, necklaces, copper bracelets and brass wire.
Mr. Benoît agrees to deliver all of the above merchandise to me, Paul Van Harp, acting on behalf of Chief Taroo.

For my commission fee, traveling expenses, etc., the aforementioned Benoît agrees to pay me the sum of 1,000 pounds in liquid money and legal tender, without prejudice to the deal struck, for having provided him with the materials necessary to repair and remast his brig.

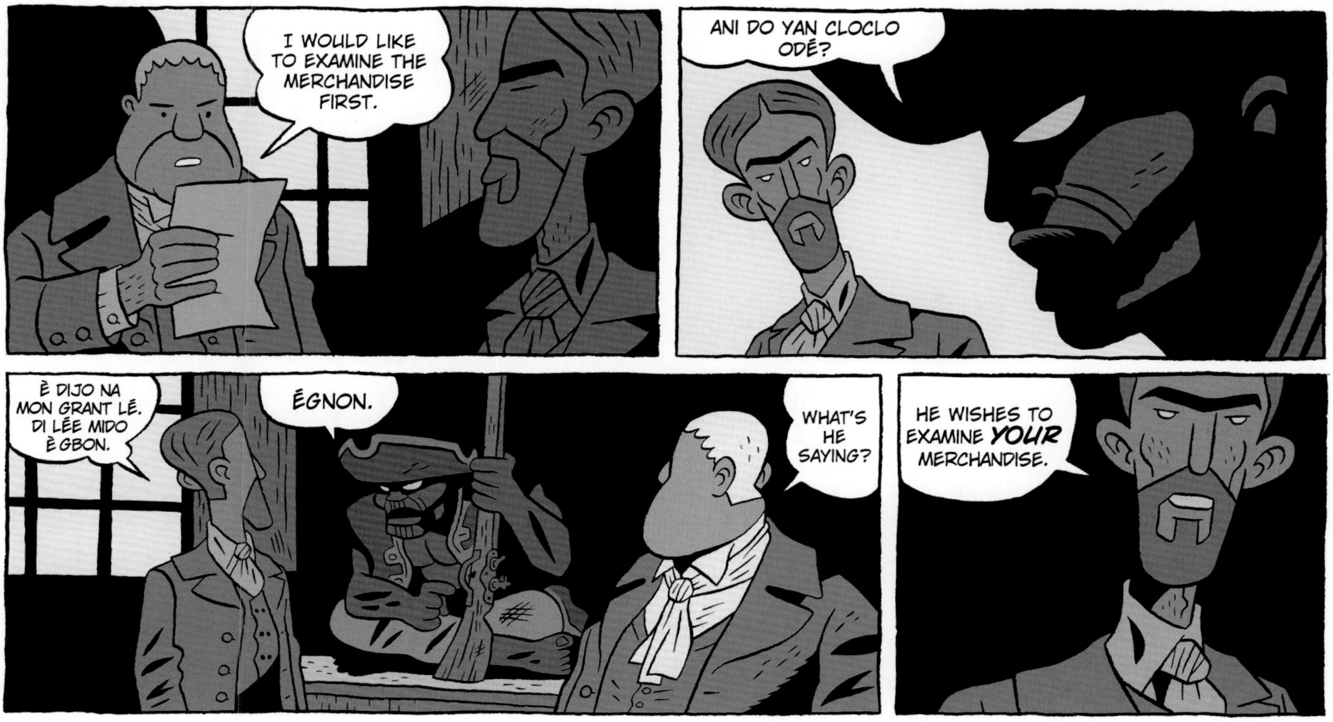

I WOULD LIKE TO EXAMINE THE MERCHANDISE FIRST.
ANI DO YAN CLOCLO ODÊ?
È DIJO NA MON GRANT LÊ. DI LÉE MIDO È GBON.
ÉGNON.
WHAT'S HE SAYING?
HE WISHES TO EXAMINE ***YOUR*** MERCHANDISE.

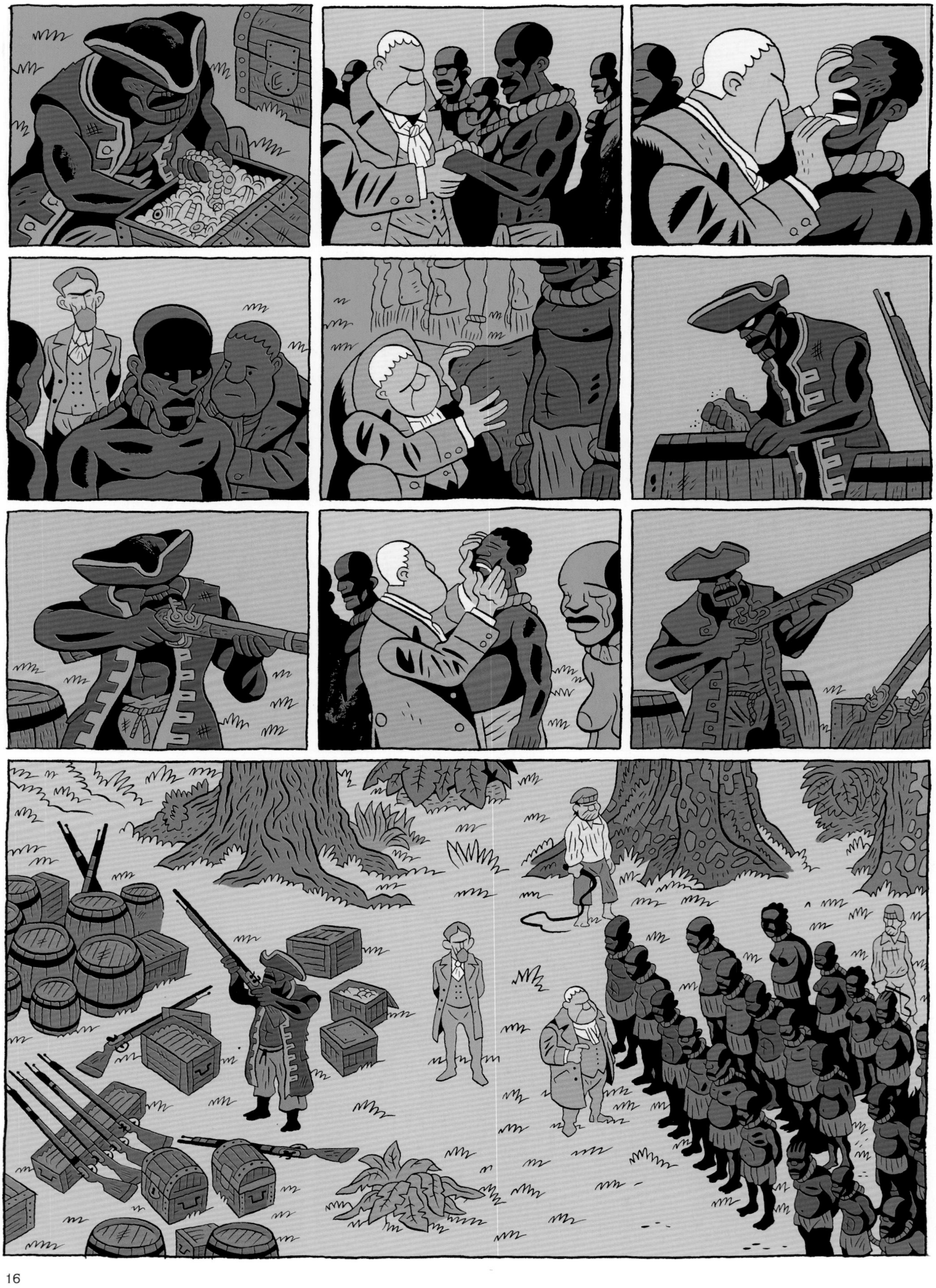

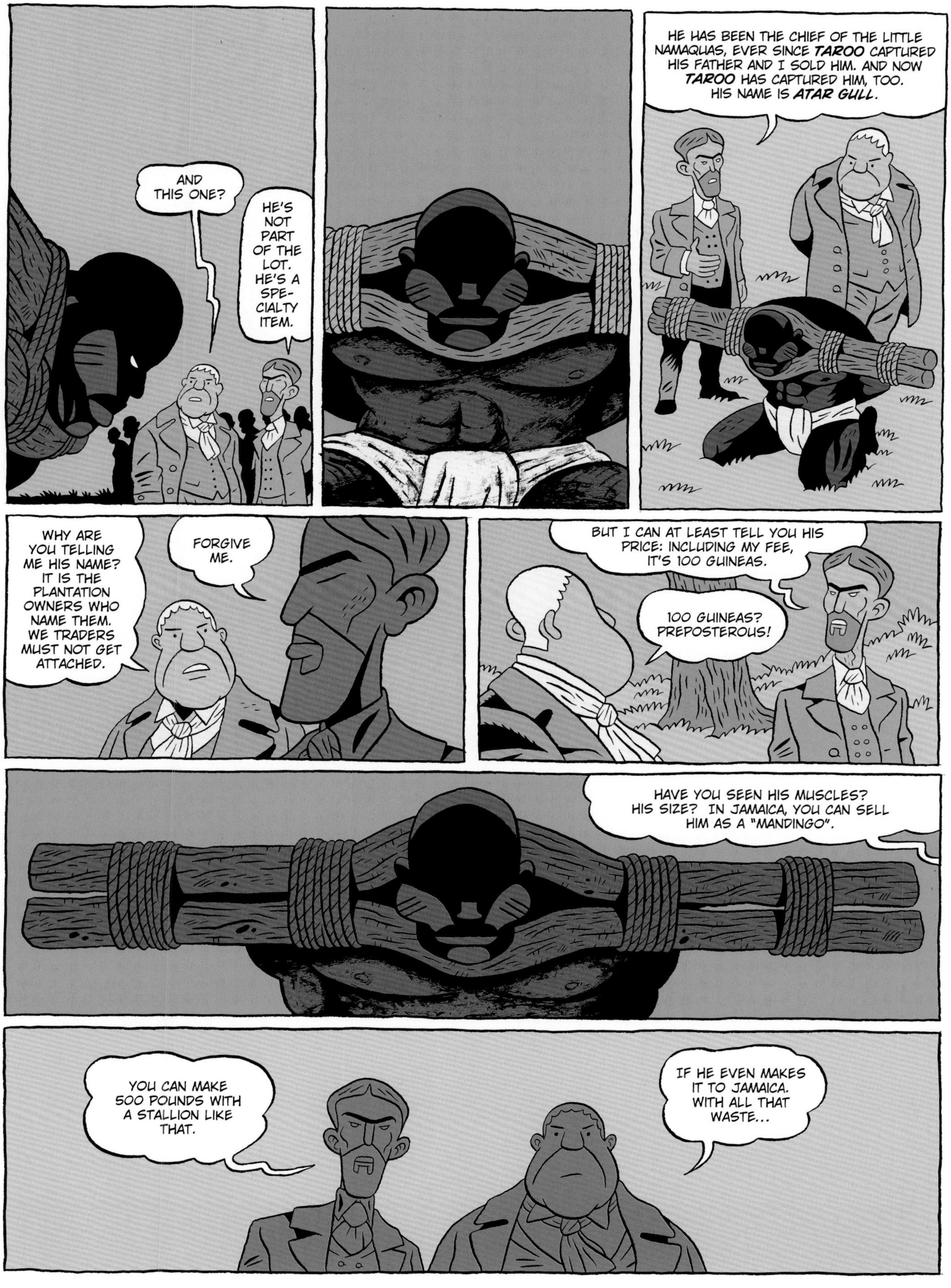

AND THIS ONE?
HE'S NOT PART OF THE LOT. HE'S A SPE-CIALTY ITEM.
HE HAS BEEN THE CHIEF OF THE LITTLE NAMAQUAS, EVER SINCE TAROO CAPTURED HIS FATHER AND I SOLD HIM. AND NOW TAROO HAS CAPTURED HIM, TOO. HIS NAME IS ATAR GULL.
WHY ARE YOU TELLING ME HIS NAME? IT IS THE PLANTATION OWNERS WHO NAME THEM. WE TRADERS MUST NOT GET ATTACHED.
FORGIVE ME.
BUT I CAN AT LEAST TELL YOU HIS PRICE: INCLUDING MY FEE, IT'S 100 GUINEAS.
100 GUINEAS? PREPOSTEROUS!
HAVE YOU SEEN HIS MUSCLES? HIS SIZE? IN JAMAICA, YOU CAN SELL HIM AS A "MANDINGO".
YOU CAN MAKE 500 POUNDS WITH A STALLION LIKE THAT.
IF HE EVEN MAKES IT TO JAMAICA. WITH ALL THAT WASTE...

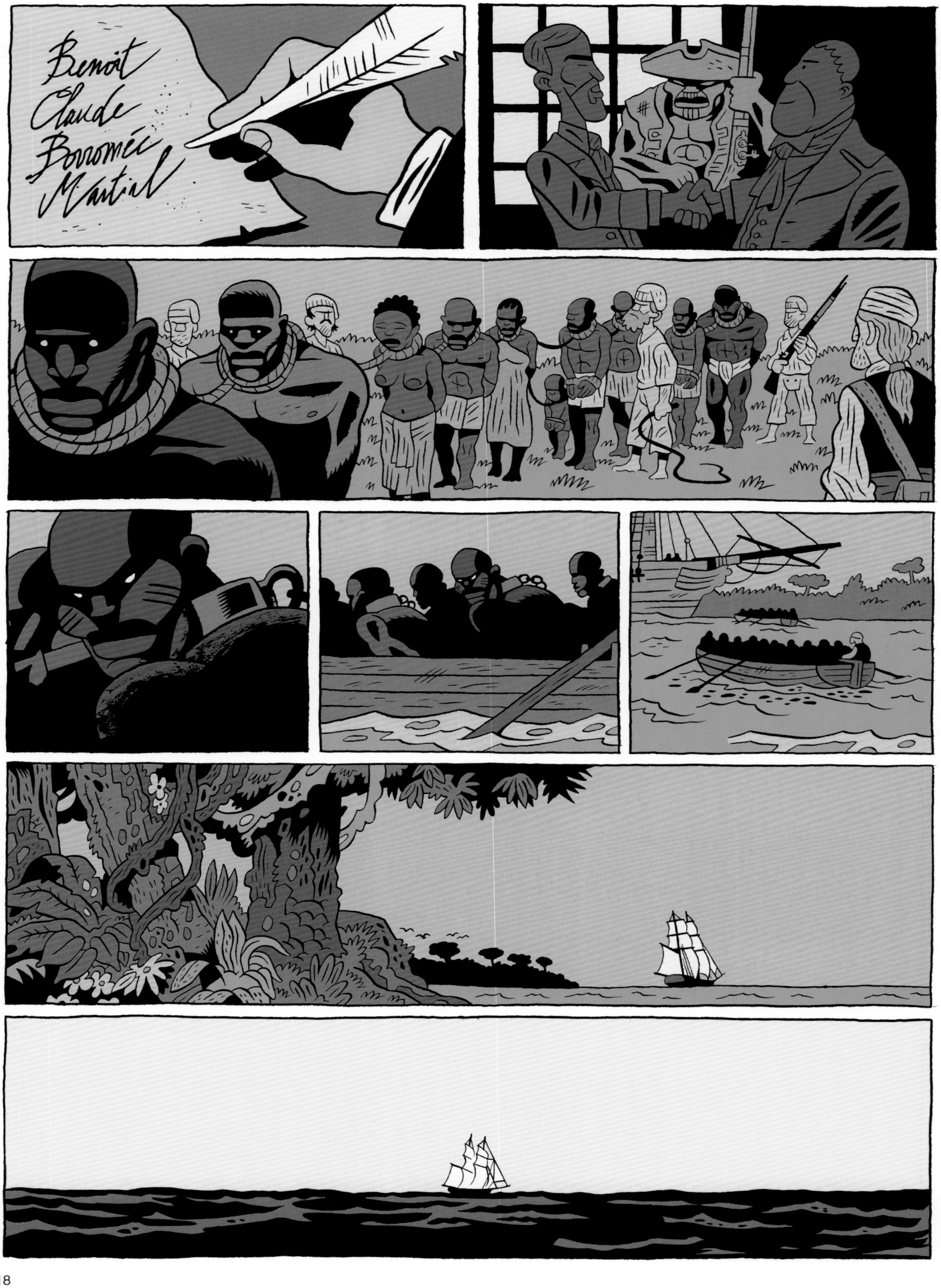
Benoît
Claude
Borromée
Martial

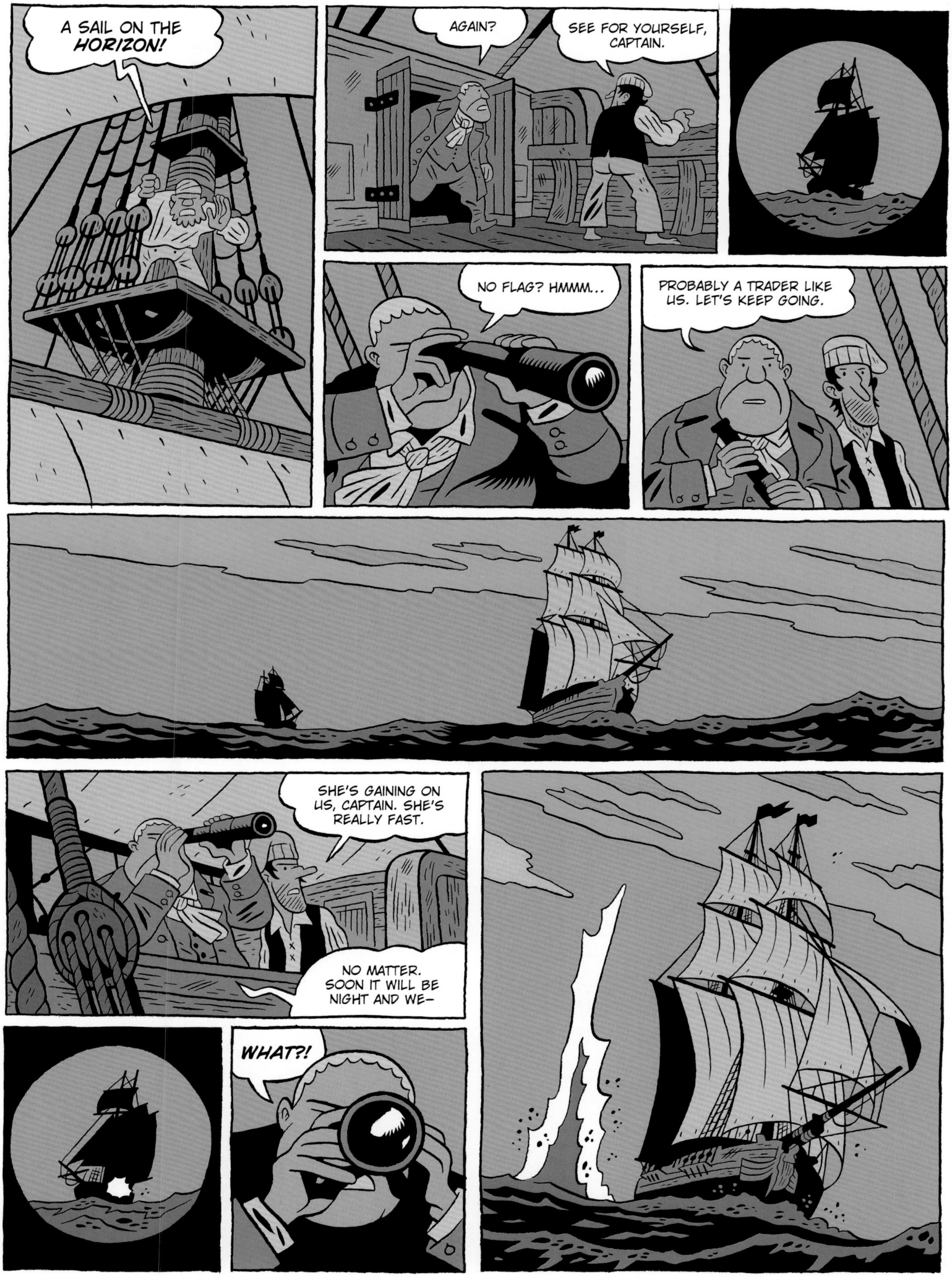
A SAIL ON THE *HORIZON!*
AGAIN?
SEE FOR YOURSELF, CAPTAIN.
NO FLAG? HMMM...
PROBABLY A TRADER LIKE US. LET'S KEEP GOING.
SHE'S GAINING ON US, CAPTAIN. SHE'S REALLY FAST.
NO MATTER. SOON IT WILL BE NIGHT AND WE–
WHAT?!

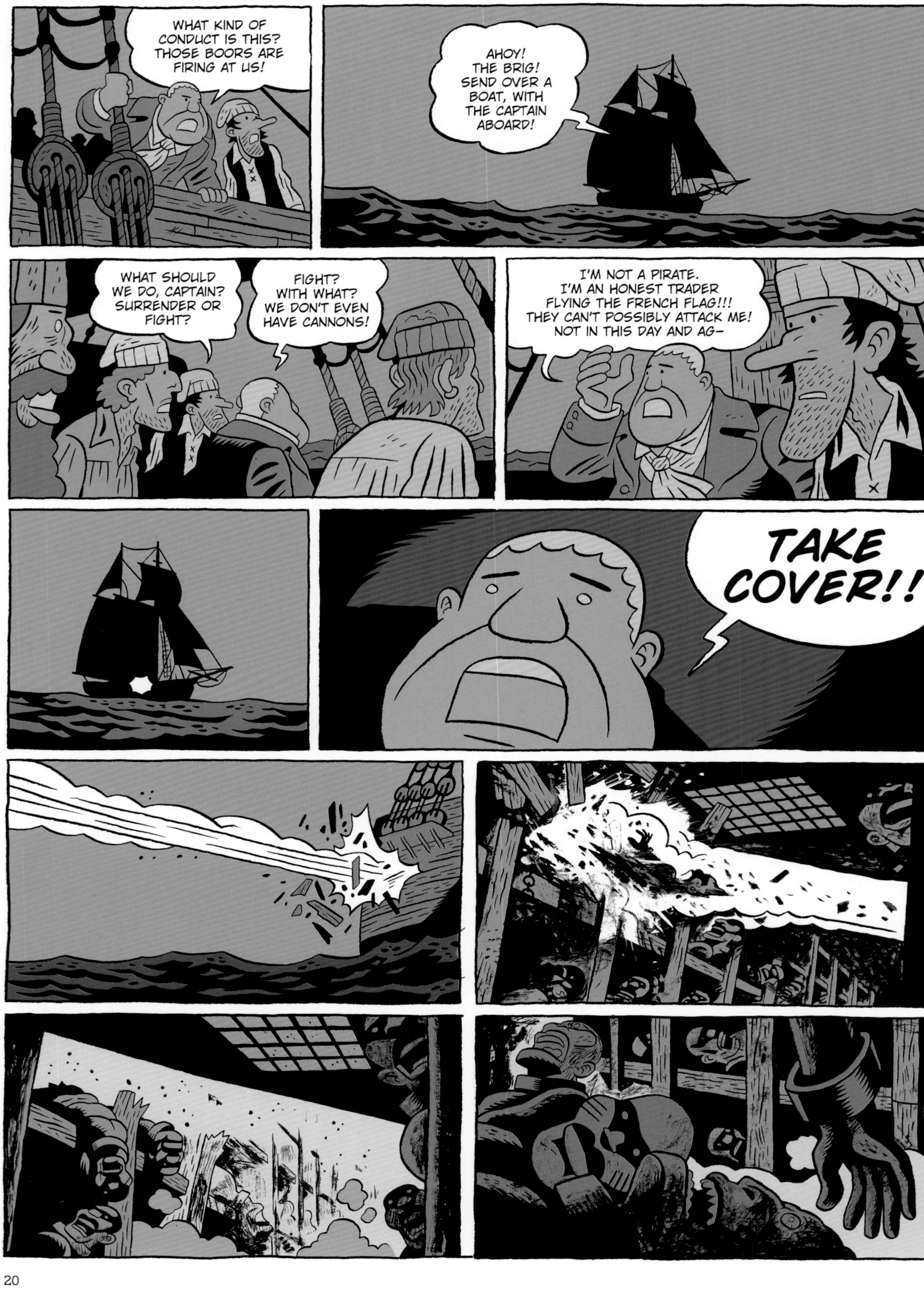
WHAT KIND OF CONDUCT IS THIS? THOSE BOORS ARE FIRING AT US!
AHOY! THE BRIG! SEND OVER A BOAT, WITH THE CAPTAIN ABOARD!
WHAT SHOULD WE DO, CAPTAIN? SURRENDER OR FIGHT?
FIGHT? WITH WHAT? WE DON'T EVEN HAVE CANNONS!
I'M NOT A PIRATE. I'M AN HONEST TRADER FLYING THE FRENCH FLAG!!! THEY CAN'T POSSIBLY ATTACK ME! NOT IN THIS DAY AND AG–
TAKE COVER!!

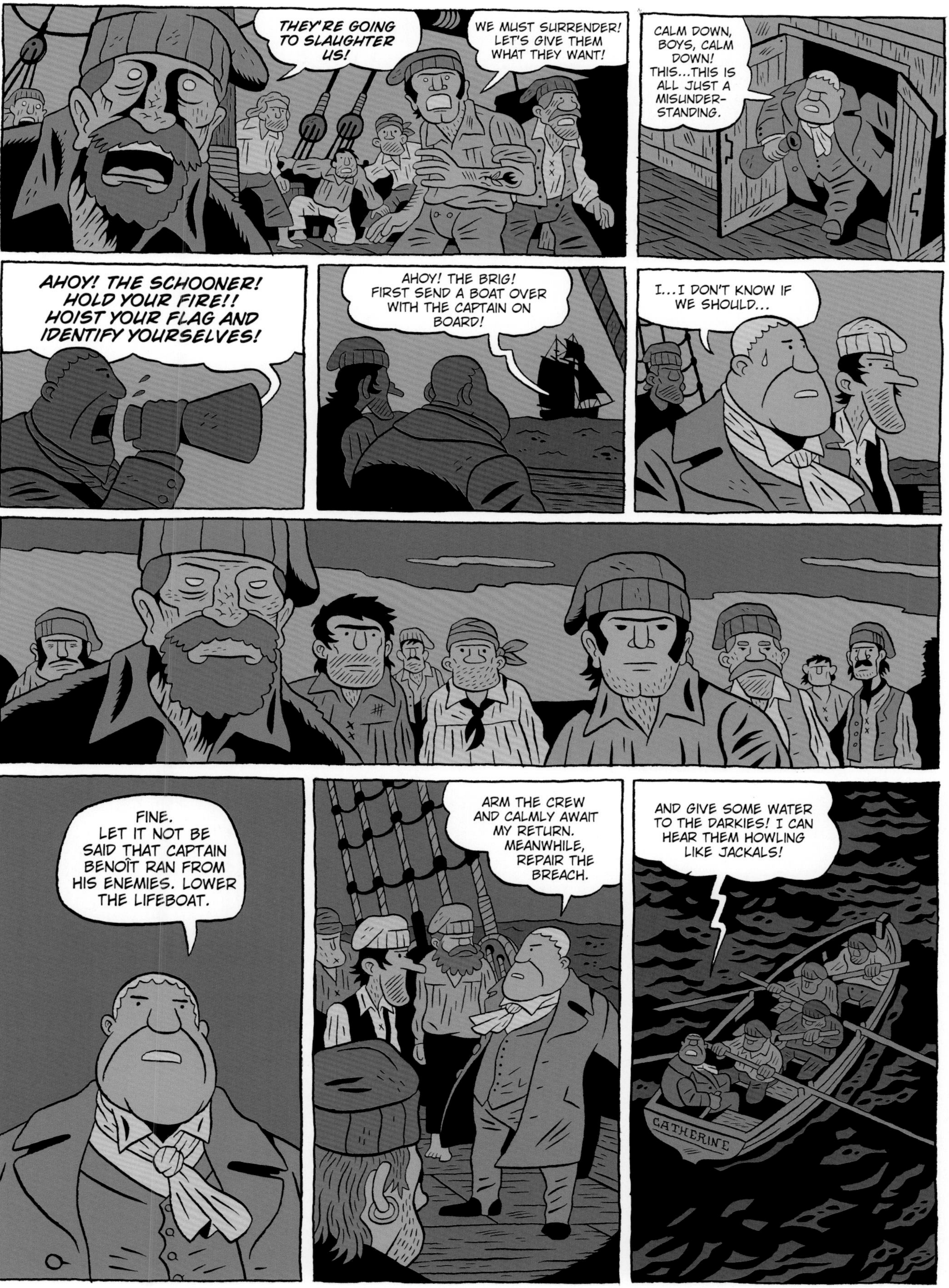
THEY'RE GOING TO SLAUGHTER US!
WE MUST SURRENDER! LET'S GIVE THEM WHAT THEY WANT!
CALM DOWN, BOYS, CALM DOWN! THIS...THIS IS ALL JUST A MISUNDER-STANDING.
AHOY! THE SCHOONER! HOLD YOUR FIRE!! HOIST YOUR FLAG AND IDENTIFY YOURSELVES!
AHOY! THE BRIG! FIRST SEND A BOAT OVER WITH THE CAPTAIN ON BOARD!
I...I DON'T KNOW IF WE SHOULD...
FINE. LET IT NOT BE SAID THAT CAPTAIN BENOÎT RAN FROM HIS ENEMIES. LOWER THE LIFEBOAT.
ARM THE CREW AND CALMLY AWAIT MY RETURN. MEANWHILE, REPAIR THE BREACH.
AND GIVE SOME WATER TO THE DARKIES! I CAN HEAR THEM HOWLING LIKE JACKALS!
CATHERINE

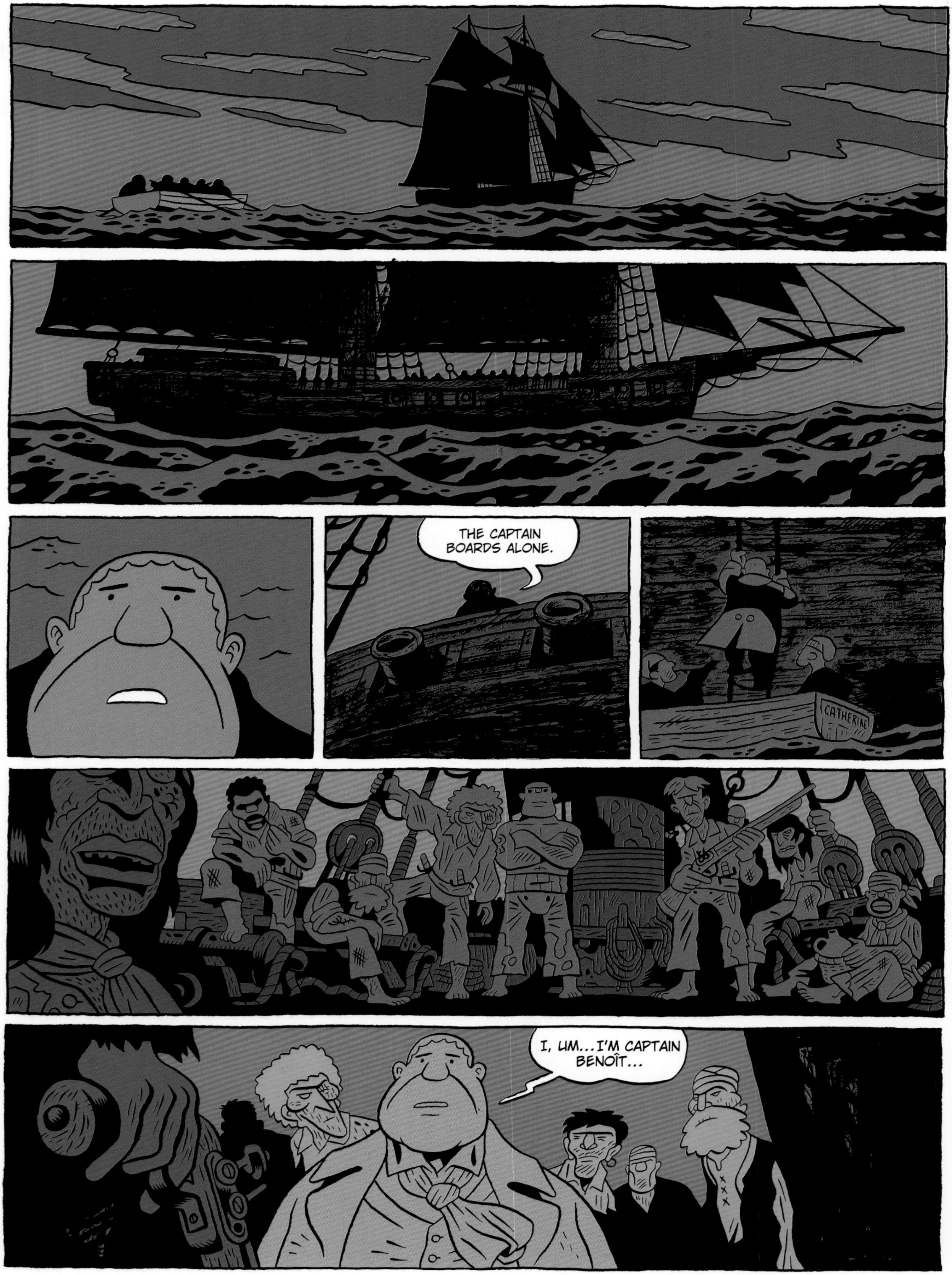
THE CAPTAIN BOARDS ALONE.
CATHERINE
I, UM...I'M CAPTAIN BENOÎT...

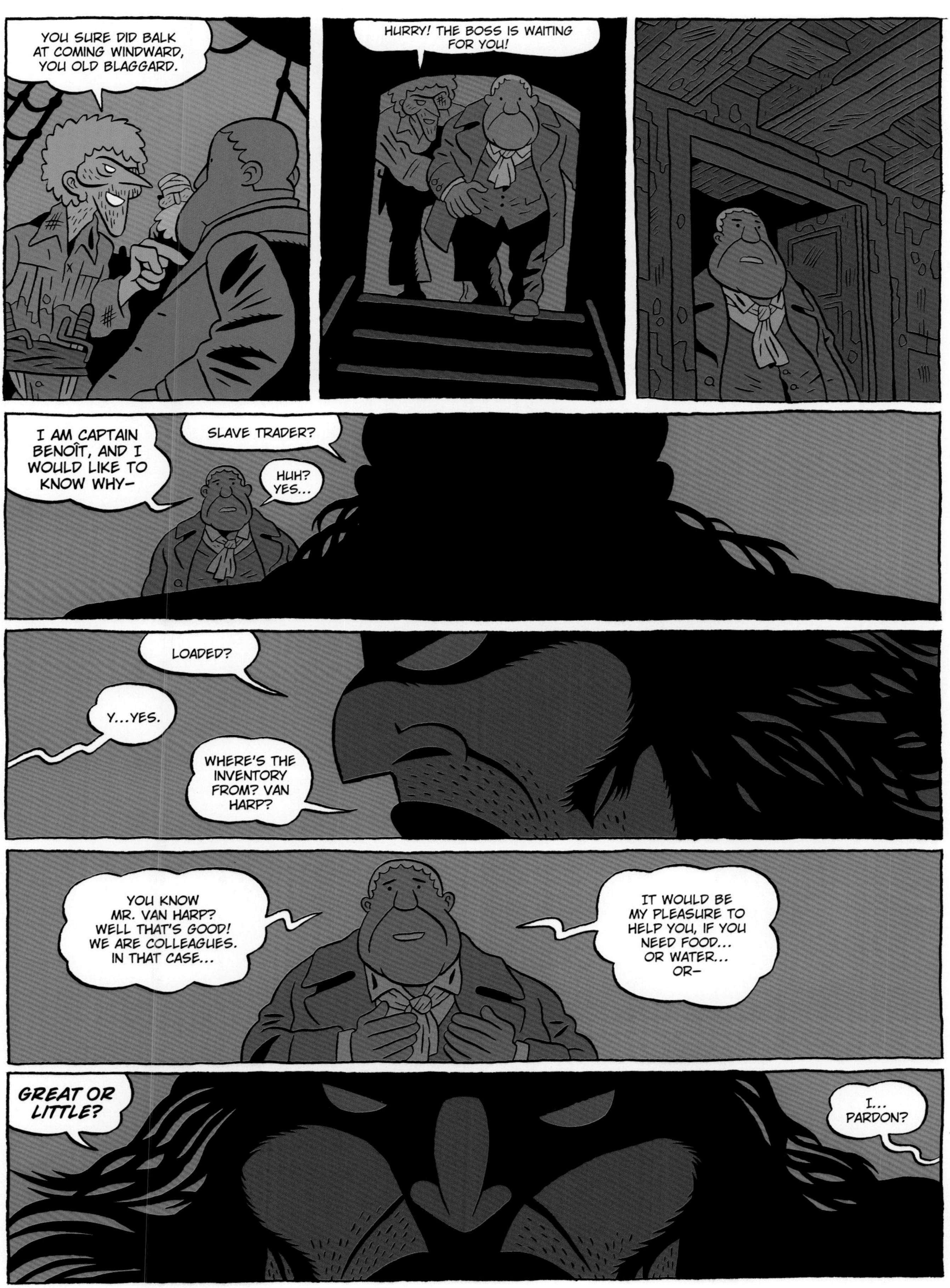
YOU SURE DID BALK AT COMING WINDWARD, YOU OLD BLAGGARD.
HURRY! THE BOSS IS WAITING FOR YOU!
I AM CAPTAIN BENOÎT, AND I WOULD LIKE TO KNOW WHY-
SLAVE TRADER?
HUH? YES...
LOADED?
Y...YES.
WHERE'S THE INVENTORY FROM? VAN HARP?
YOU KNOW MR. VAN HARP? WELL THAT'S GOOD! WE ARE COLLEAGUES. IN THAT CASE...
IT WOULD BE MY PLEASURE TO HELP YOU, IF YOU NEED FOOD... OR WATER... OR-
GREAT OR LITTLE?
I... PARDON?

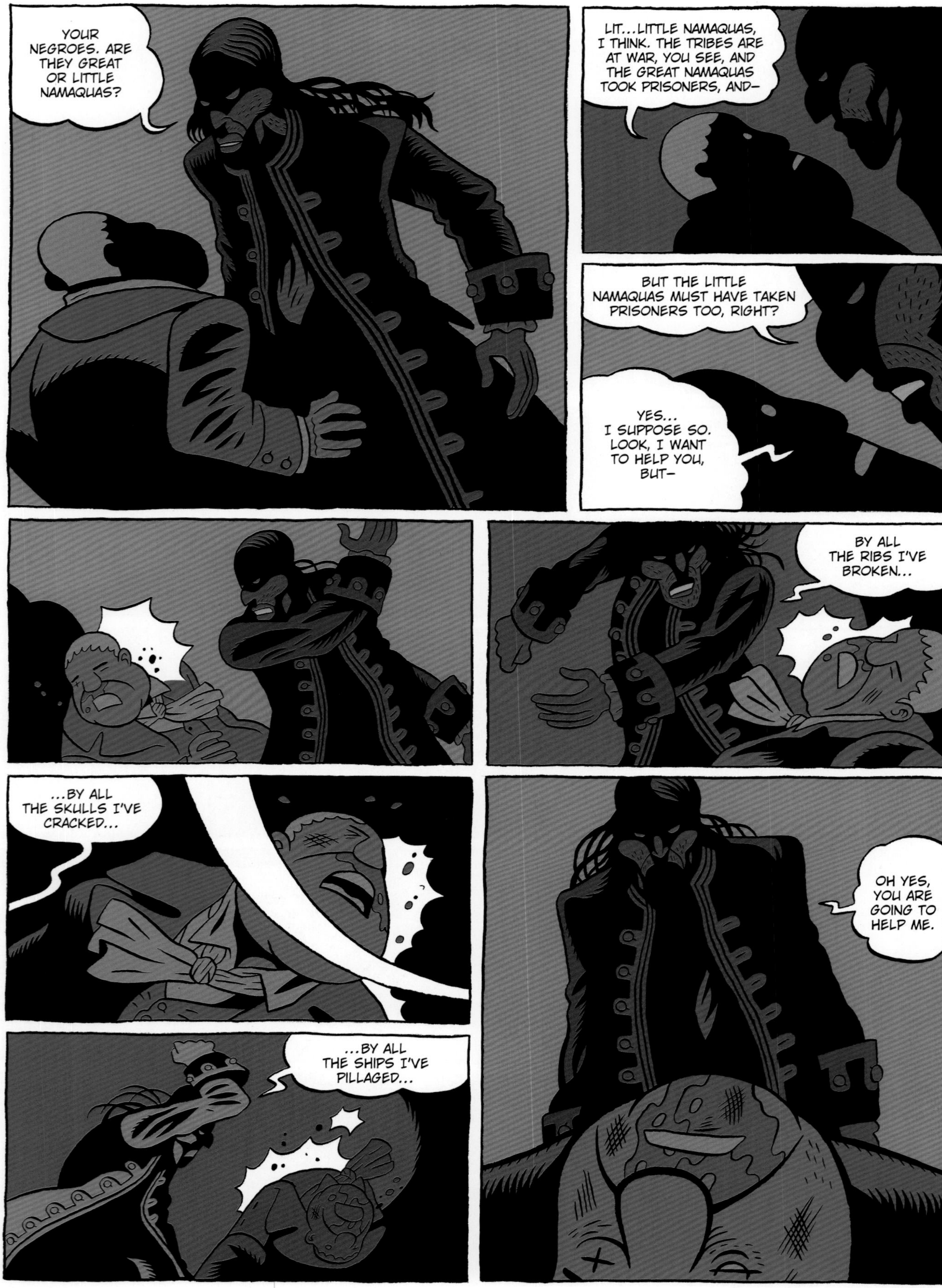
YOUR NEGROES. ARE THEY GREAT OR LITTLE NAMAQUAS?
LIT...LITTLE NAMAQUAS, I THINK. THE TRIBES ARE AT WAR, YOU SEE, AND THE GREAT NAMAQUAS TOOK PRISONERS, AND–
BUT THE LITTLE NAMAQUAS MUST HAVE TAKEN PRISONERS TOO, RIGHT?
YES... I SUPPOSE SO. LOOK, I WANT TO HELP YOU, BUT–
BY ALL THE RIBS I'VE BROKEN...
...BY ALL THE SKULLS I'VE CRACKED...
...BY ALL THE SHIPS I'VE PILLAGED...
OH YES, YOU ARE GOING TO HELP ME.

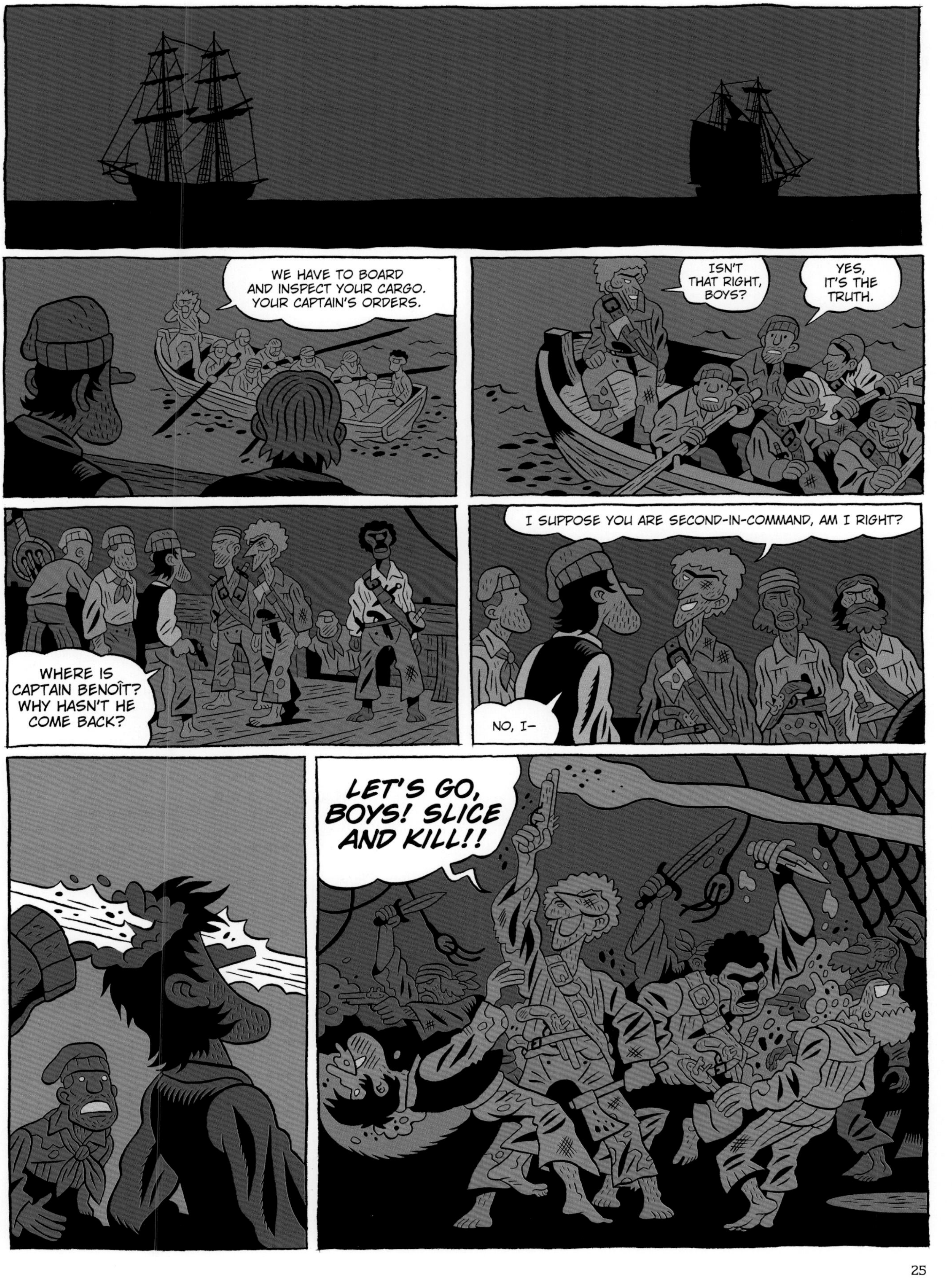
WE HAVE TO BOARD AND INSPECT YOUR CARGO. YOUR CAPTAIN'S ORDERS.
ISN'T THAT RIGHT, BOYS?
YES, IT'S THE TRUTH.
WHERE IS CAPTAIN BENOÎT? WHY HASN'T HE COME BACK?
I SUPPOSE YOU ARE SECOND-IN-COMMAND, AM I RIGHT?
NO, I–
LET'S GO, BOYS! SLICE AND KILL!!

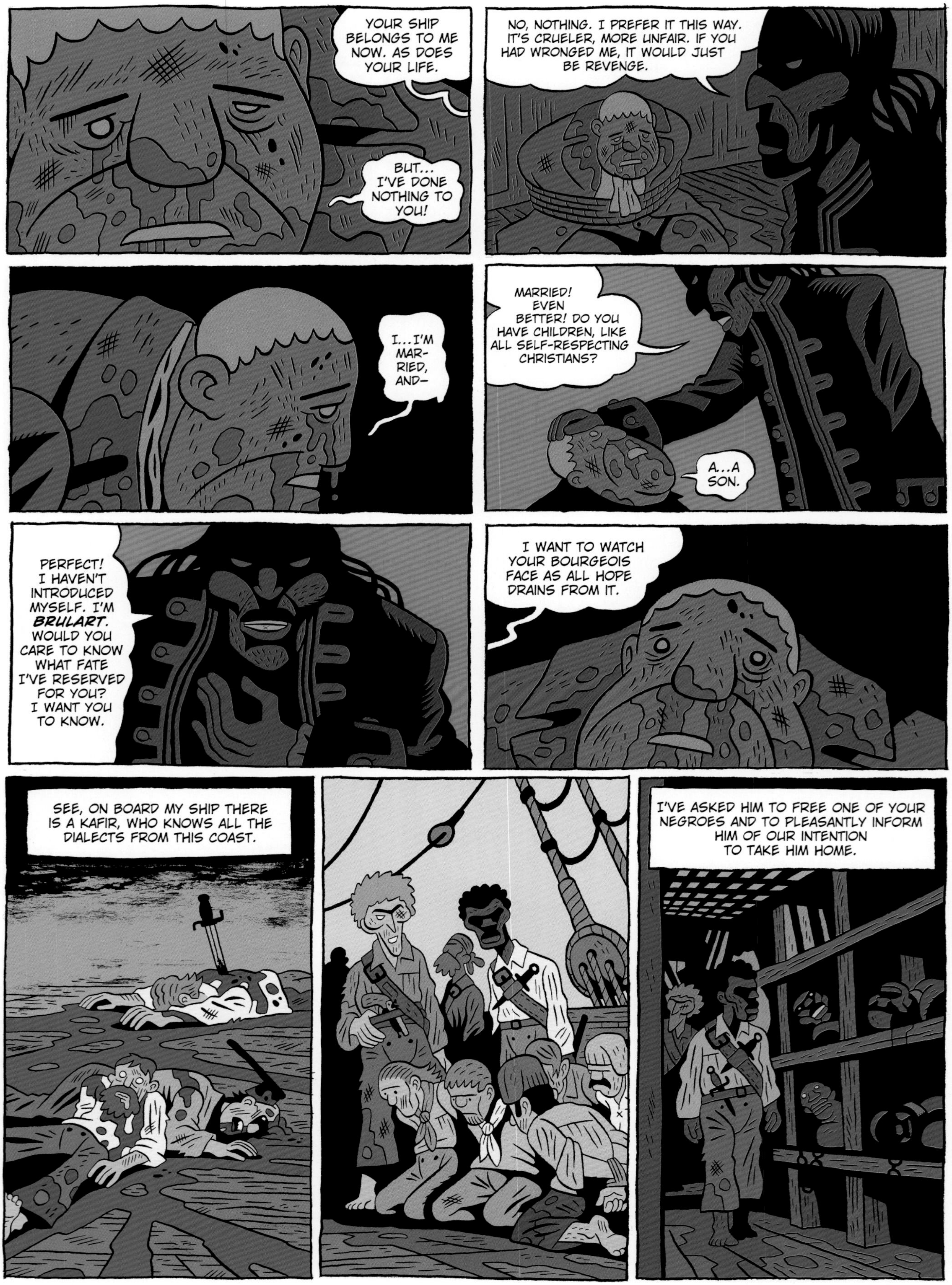
YOUR SHIP BELONGS TO ME NOW. AS DOES YOUR LIFE.
BUT... I'VE DONE NOTHING TO YOU!
NO, NOTHING. I PREFER IT THIS WAY. IT'S CRUELER, MORE UNFAIR. IF YOU HAD WRONGED ME, IT WOULD JUST BE REVENGE.
I...I'M MAR-RIED, AND–
MARRIED! EVEN BETTER! DO YOU HAVE CHILDREN, LIKE ALL SELF-RESPECTING CHRISTIANS?
A...A SON.
PERFECT! I HAVEN'T INTRODUCED MYSELF. I'M **BRULART**. WOULD YOU CARE TO KNOW WHAT FATE I'VE RESERVED FOR YOU? I WANT YOU TO KNOW.
I WANT TO WATCH YOUR BOURGEOIS FACE AS ALL HOPE DRAINS FROM IT.
SEE, ON BOARD MY SHIP THERE IS A KAFIR, WHO KNOWS ALL THE DIALECTS FROM THIS COAST.
I'VE ASKED HIM TO FREE ONE OF YOUR NEGROES AND TO PLEASANTLY INFORM HIM OF OUR INTENTION TO TAKE HIM HOME.

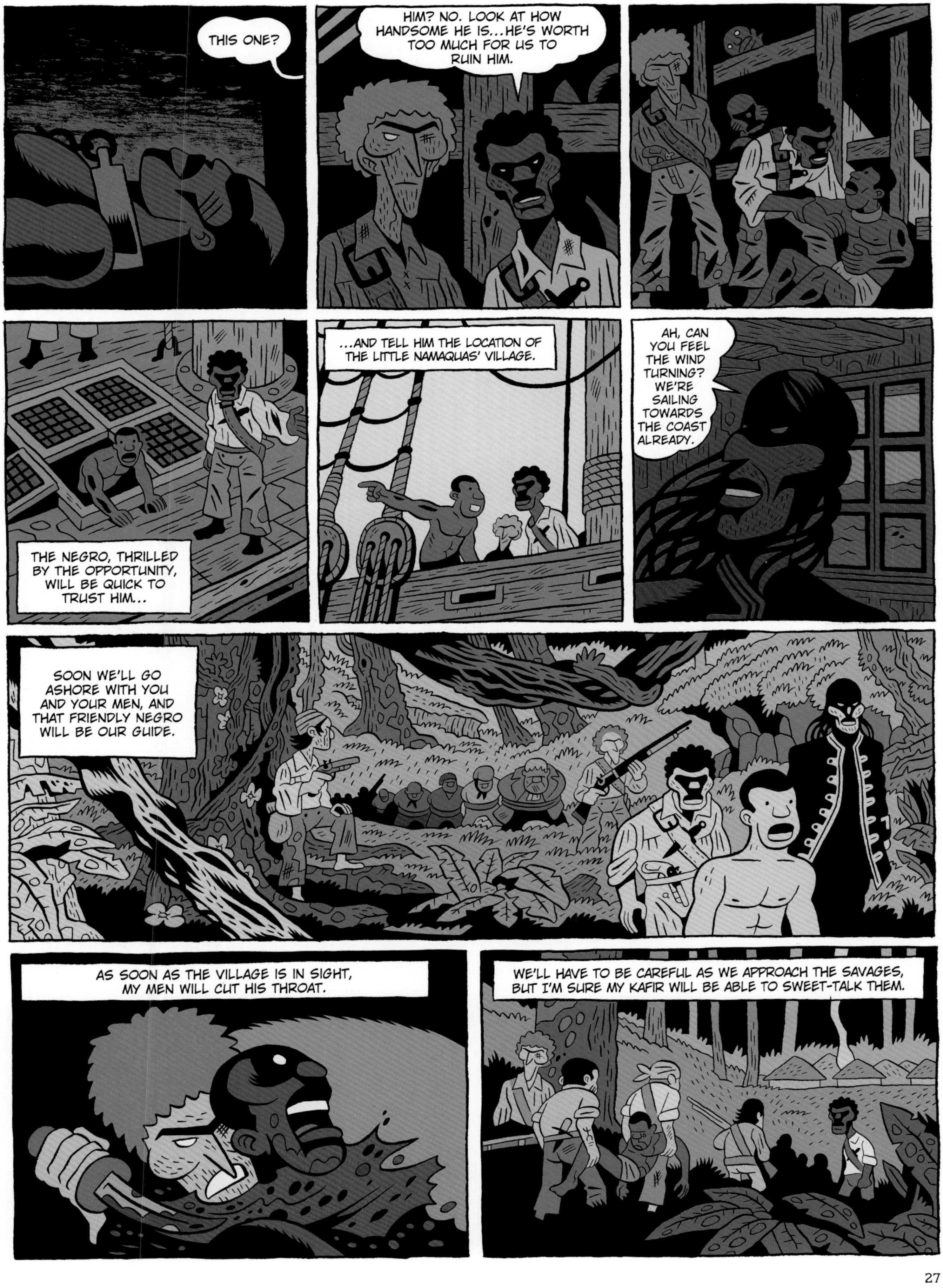
THIS ONE?
HIM? NO. LOOK AT HOW HANDSOME HE IS...HE'S WORTH TOO MUCH FOR US TO RUIN HIM.
THE NEGRO, THRILLED BY THE OPPORTUNITY, WILL BE QUICK TO TRUST HIM...
...AND TELL HIM THE LOCATION OF THE LITTLE NAMAQUAS' VILLAGE.
AH, CAN YOU FEEL THE WIND TURNING? WE'RE SAILING TOWARDS THE COAST ALREADY.
SOON WE'LL GO ASHORE WITH YOU AND YOUR MEN, AND THAT FRIENDLY NEGRO WILL BE OUR GUIDE.
AS SOON AS THE VILLAGE IS IN SIGHT, MY MEN WILL CUT HIS THROAT.
WE'LL HAVE TO BE CAREFUL AS WE APPROACH THE SAVAGES, BUT I'M SURE MY KAFIR WILL BE ABLE TO SWEET-TALK THEM.

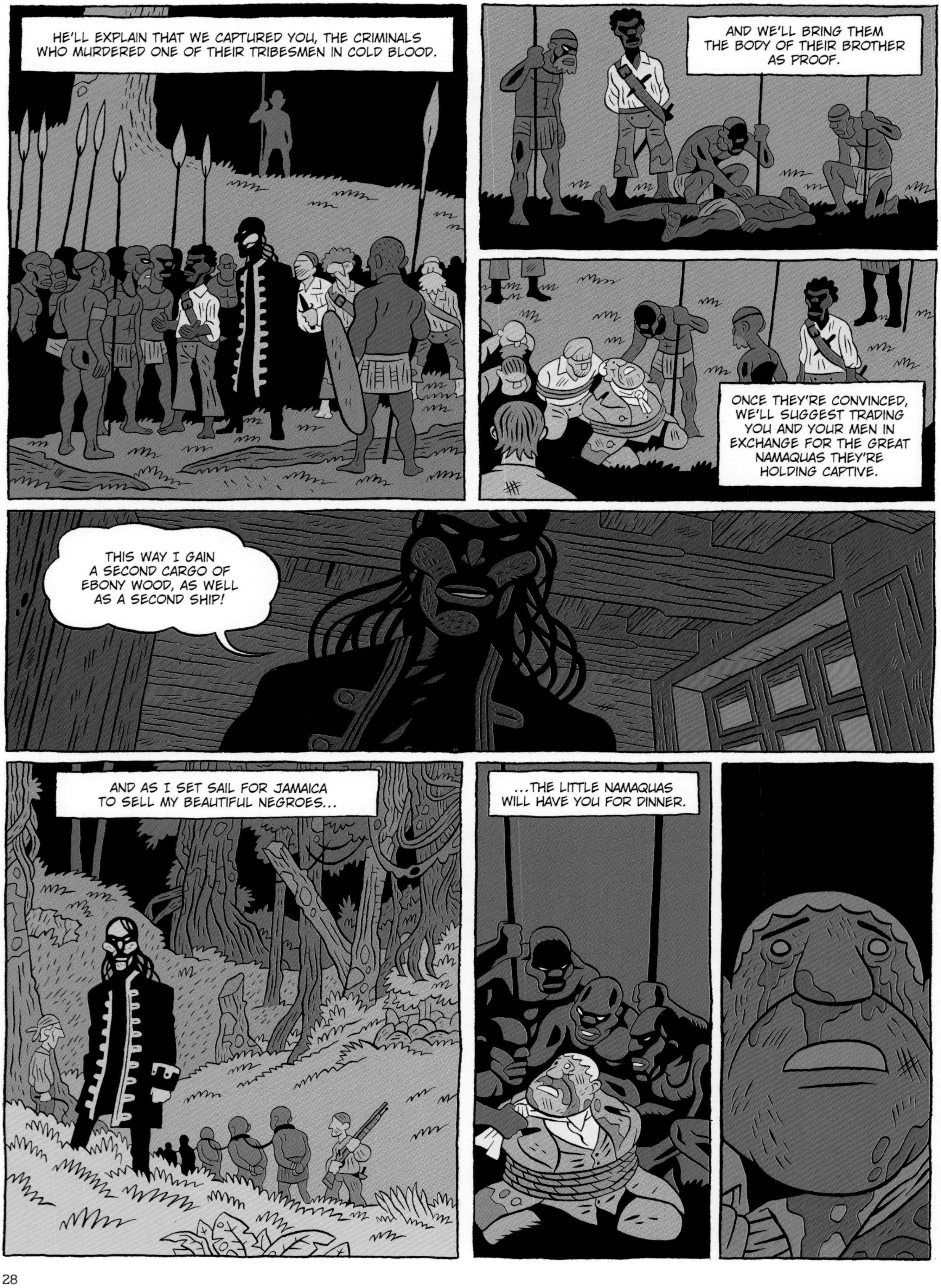
HE'LL EXPLAIN THAT WE CAPTURED YOU, THE CRIMINALS WHO MURDERED ONE OF THEIR TRIBESMEN IN COLD BLOOD.
AND WE'LL BRING THEM THE BODY OF THEIR BROTHER AS PROOF.
ONCE THEY'RE CONVINCED, WE'LL SUGGEST TRADING YOU AND YOUR MEN IN EXCHANGE FOR THE GREAT NAMAQUAS THEY'RE HOLDING CAPTIVE.
THIS WAY I GAIN A SECOND CARGO OF EBONY WOOD, AS WELL AS A SECOND SHIP!
AND AS I SET SAIL FOR JAMAICA TO SELL MY BEAUTIFUL NEGROES...
...THE LITTLE NAMAQUAS WILL HAVE YOU FOR DINNER.

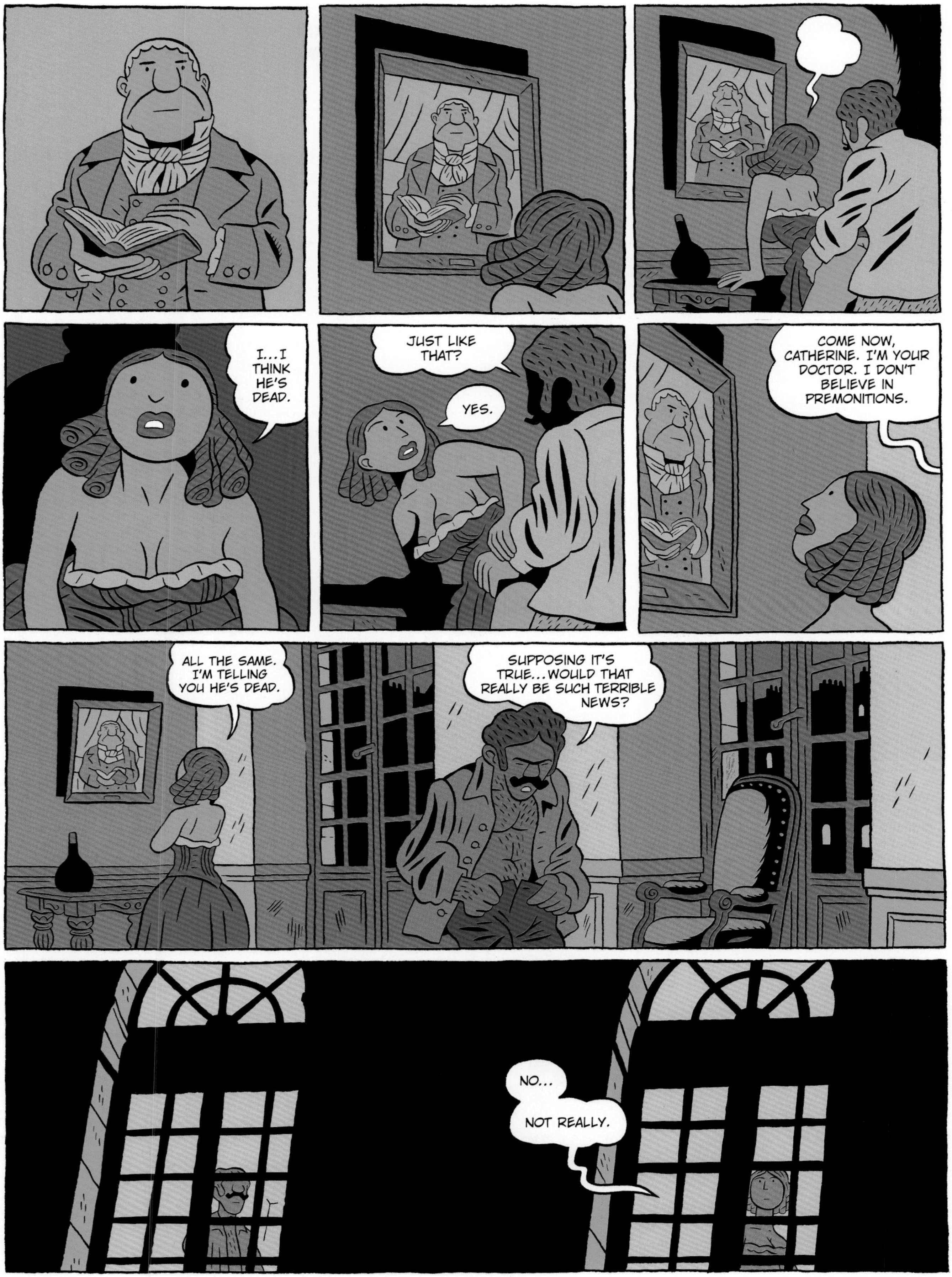

I...I THINK HE'S DEAD.
JUST LIKE THAT?
YES.
COME NOW, CATHERINE. I'M YOUR DOCTOR. I DON'T BELIEVE IN PREMONITIONS.
ALL THE SAME. I'M TELLING YOU HE'S DEAD.
SUPPOSING IT'S TRUE...WOULD THAT REALLY BE SUCH TERRIBLE NEWS?
NO...
NOT REALLY.

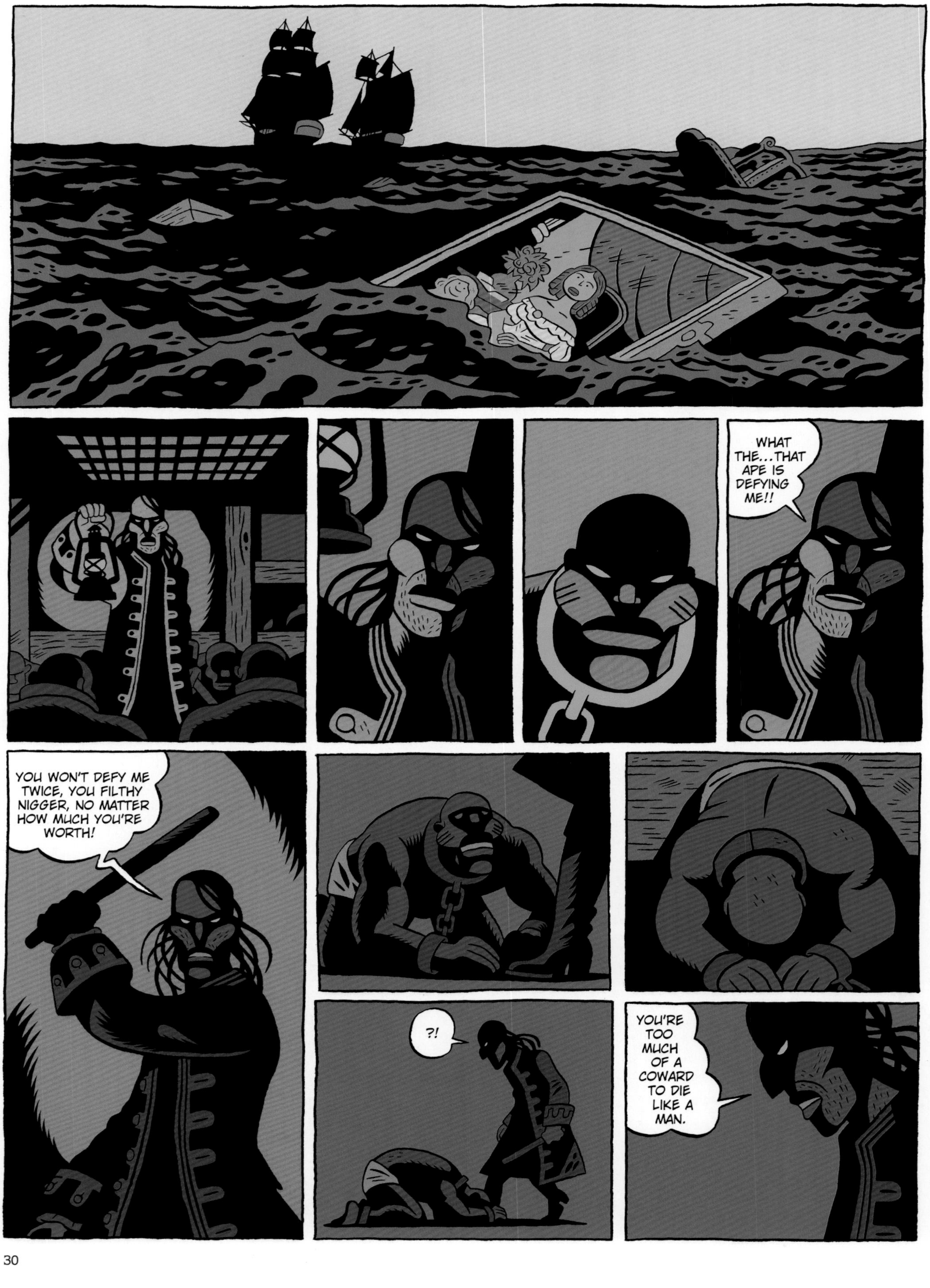
WHAT THE...THAT APE IS DEFYING ME!!
YOU WON'T DEFY ME TWICE, YOU FILTHY NIGGER, NO MATTER HOW MUCH YOU'RE WORTH!
?!
YOU'RE TOO MUCH OF A COWARD TO DIE LIKE A MAN.

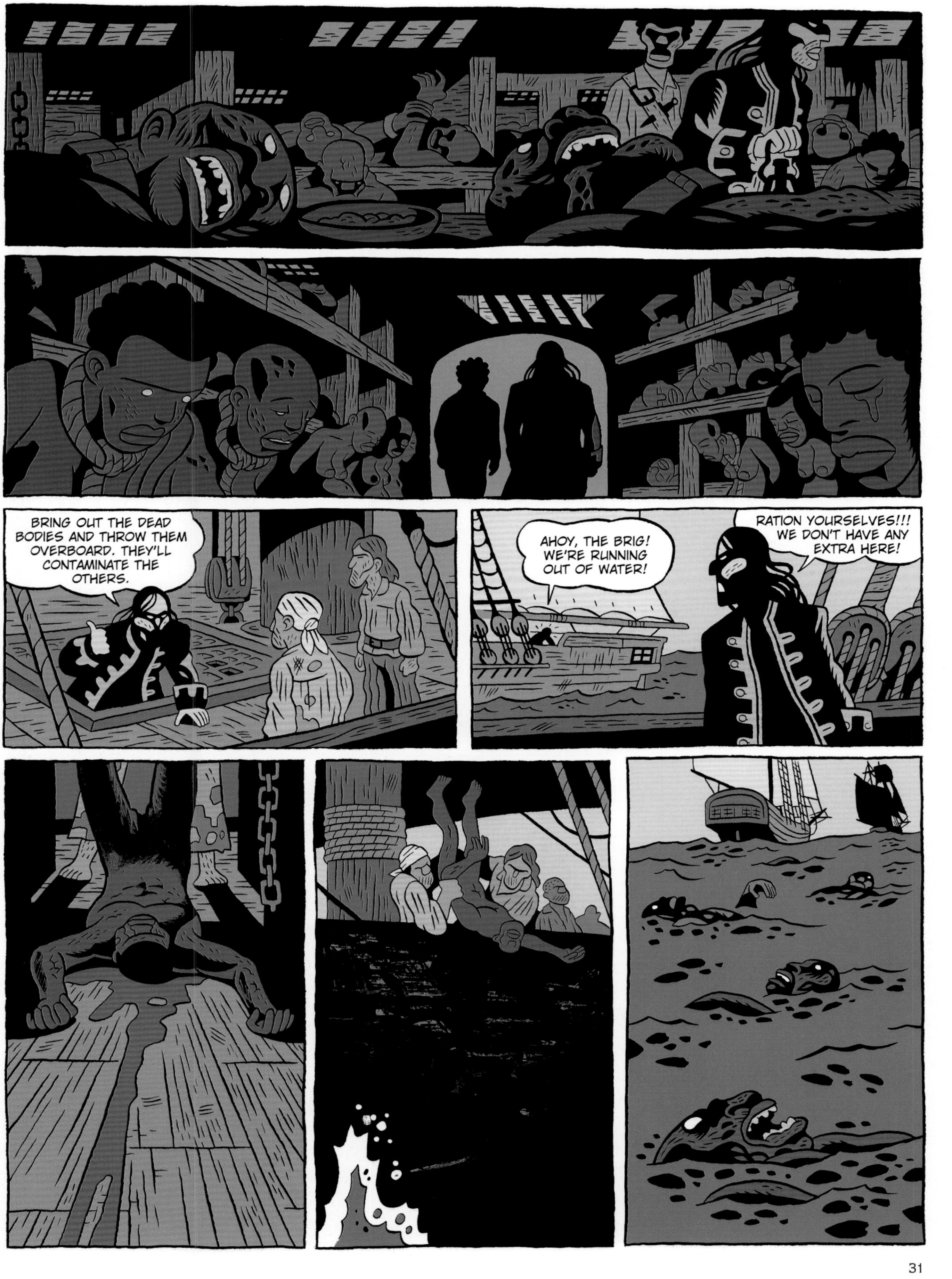
BRING OUT THE DEAD BODIES AND THROW THEM OVERBOARD. THEY'LL CONTAMINATE THE OTHERS.
AHOY, THE BRIG! WE'RE RUNNING OUT OF WATER!
RATION YOURSELVES!!! WE DON'T HAVE ANY EXTRA HERE!

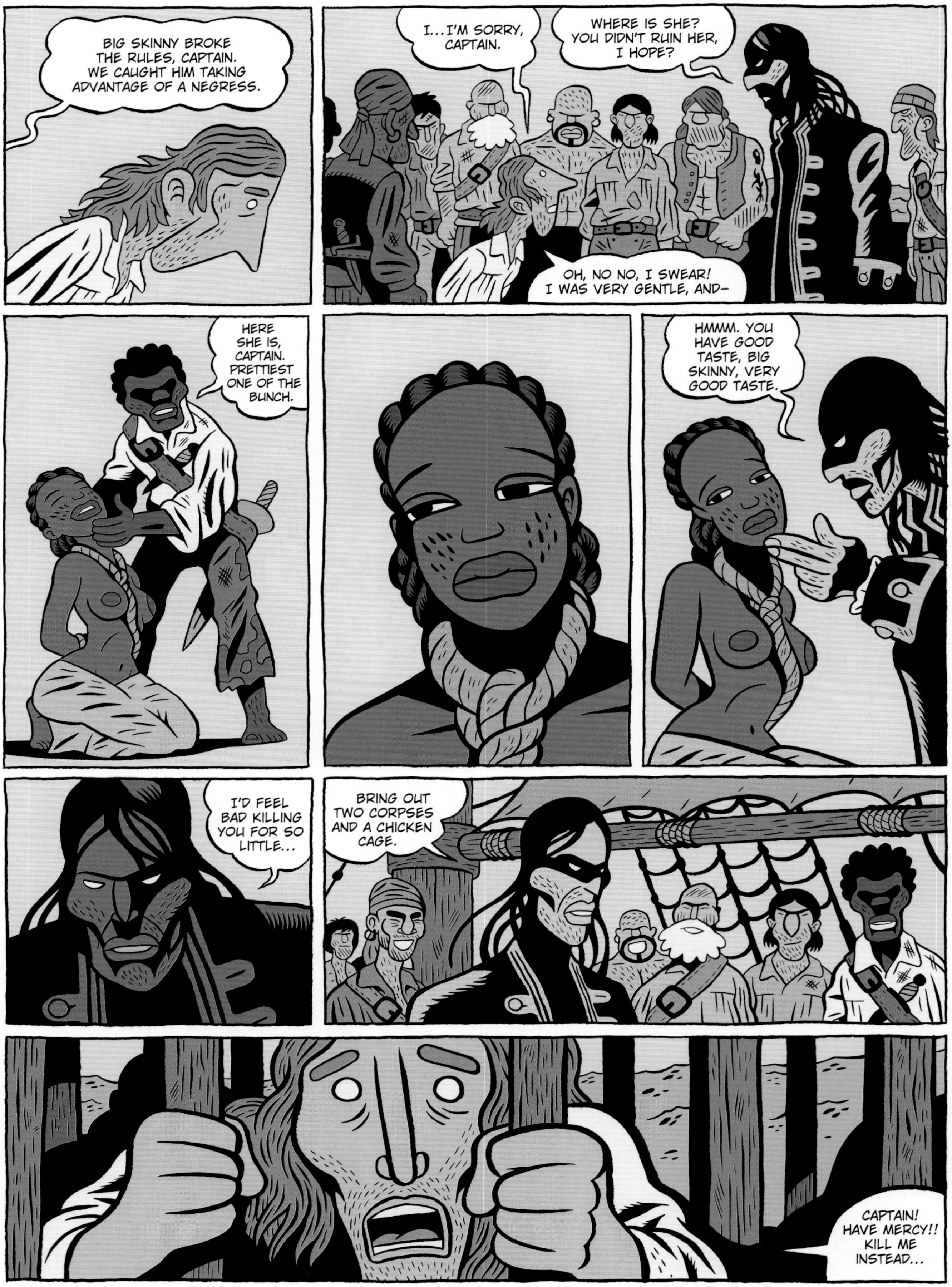
BIG SKINNY BROKE THE RULES, CAPTAIN. WE CAUGHT HIM TAKING ADVANTAGE OF A NEGRESS.
I...I'M SORRY, CAPTAIN.
WHERE IS SHE? YOU DIDN'T RUIN HER, I HOPE?
OH, NO NO, I SWEAR! I WAS VERY GENTLE, AND–
HERE SHE IS, CAPTAIN. PRETTIEST ONE OF THE BUNCH.
HMMM. YOU HAVE GOOD TASTE, BIG SKINNY, VERY GOOD TASTE.
I'D FEEL BAD KILLING YOU FOR SO LITTLE...
BRING OUT TWO CORPSES AND A CHICKEN CAGE.
CAPTAIN! HAVE MERCY!! KILL ME INSTEAD...

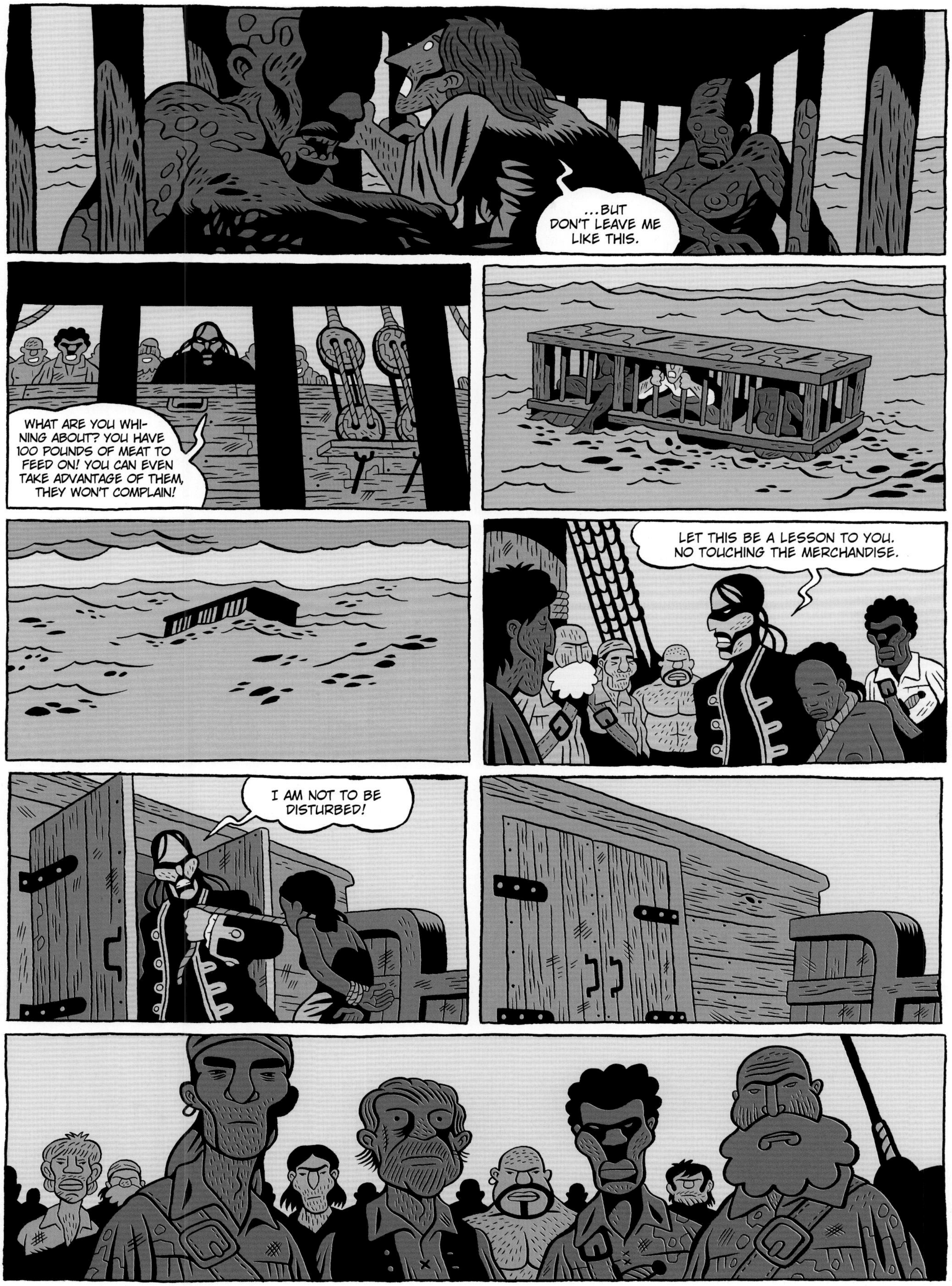
...BUT DON'T LEAVE ME LIKE THIS.
WHAT ARE YOU WHINING ABOUT? YOU HAVE 100 POUNDS OF MEAT TO FEED ON! YOU CAN EVEN TAKE ADVANTAGE OF THEM, THEY WON'T COMPLAIN!
LET THIS BE A LESSON TO YOU. NO TOUCHING THE MERCHANDISE.
I AM NOT TO BE DISTURBED!

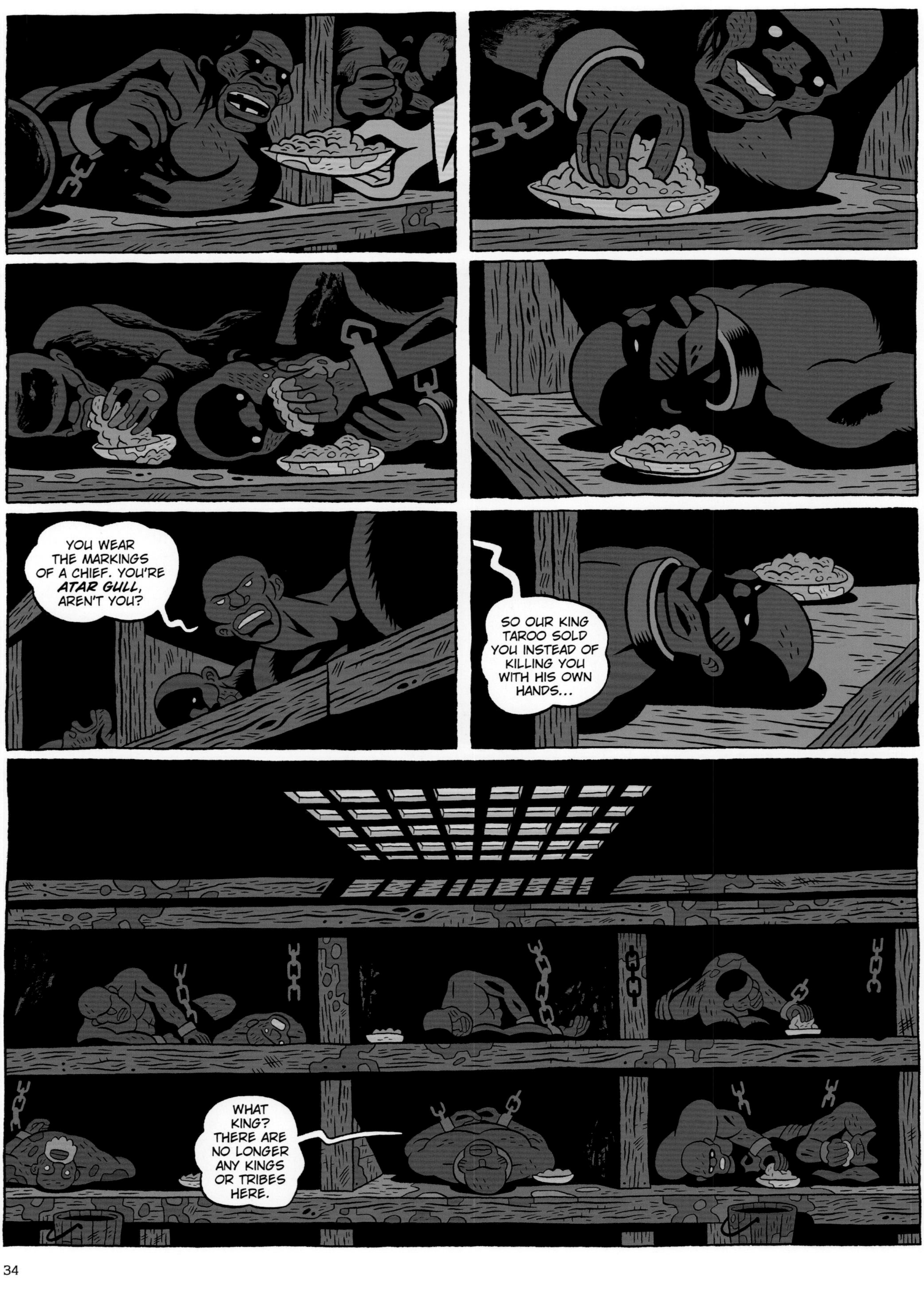
YOU WEAR THE MARKINGS OF A CHIEF. YOU'RE ATAR GULL, AREN'T YOU?
SO OUR KING TAROO SOLD YOU INSTEAD OF KILLING YOU WITH HIS OWN HANDS...
WHAT KING? THERE ARE NO LONGER ANY KINGS OR TRIBES HERE.

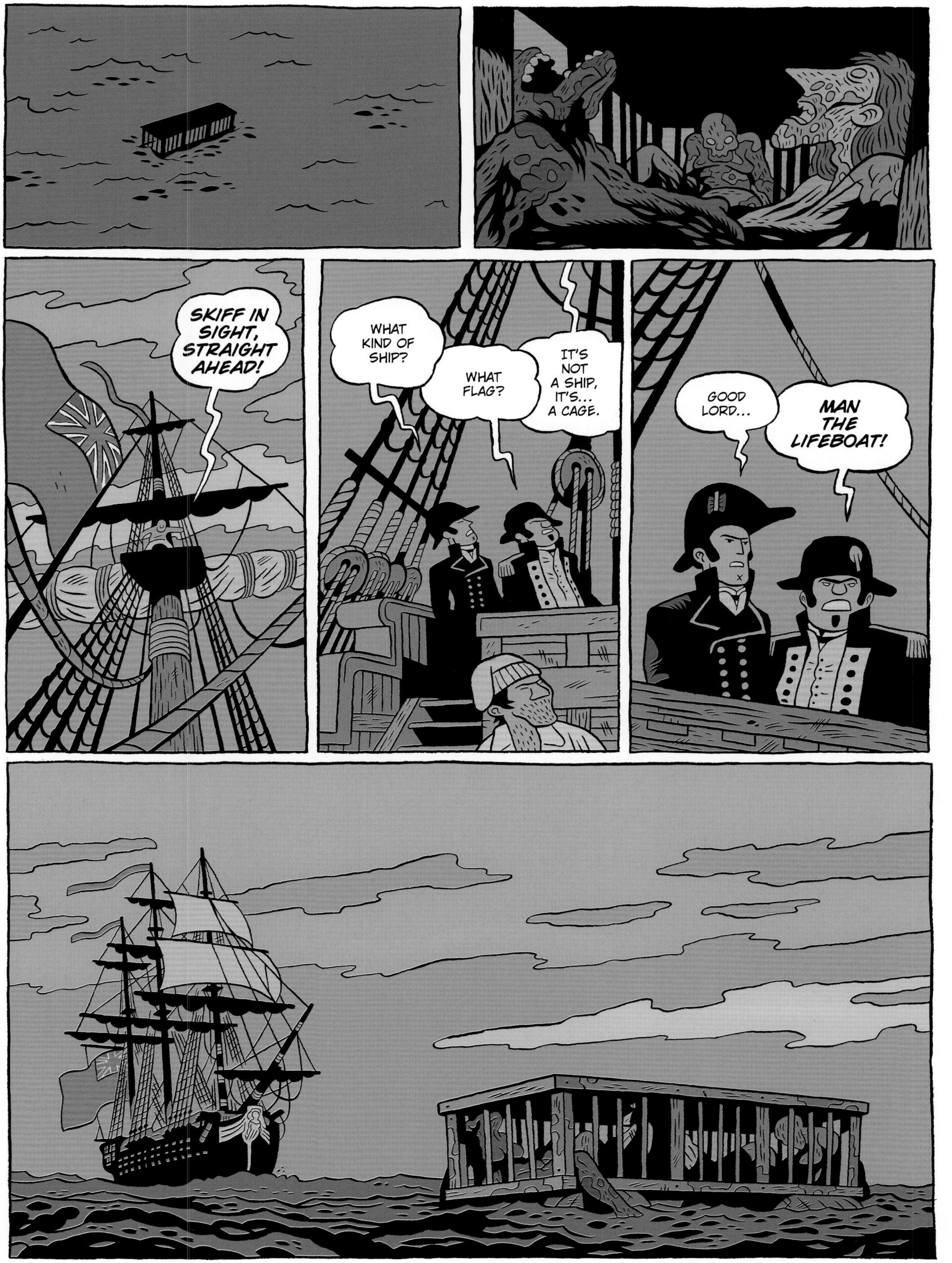
SKIFF IN SIGHT, STRAIGHT AHEAD!
WHAT KIND OF SHIP?
WHAT FLAG?
IT'S NOT A SHIP, IT'S... A CAGE.
GOOD LORD...
MAN THE LIFEBOAT!

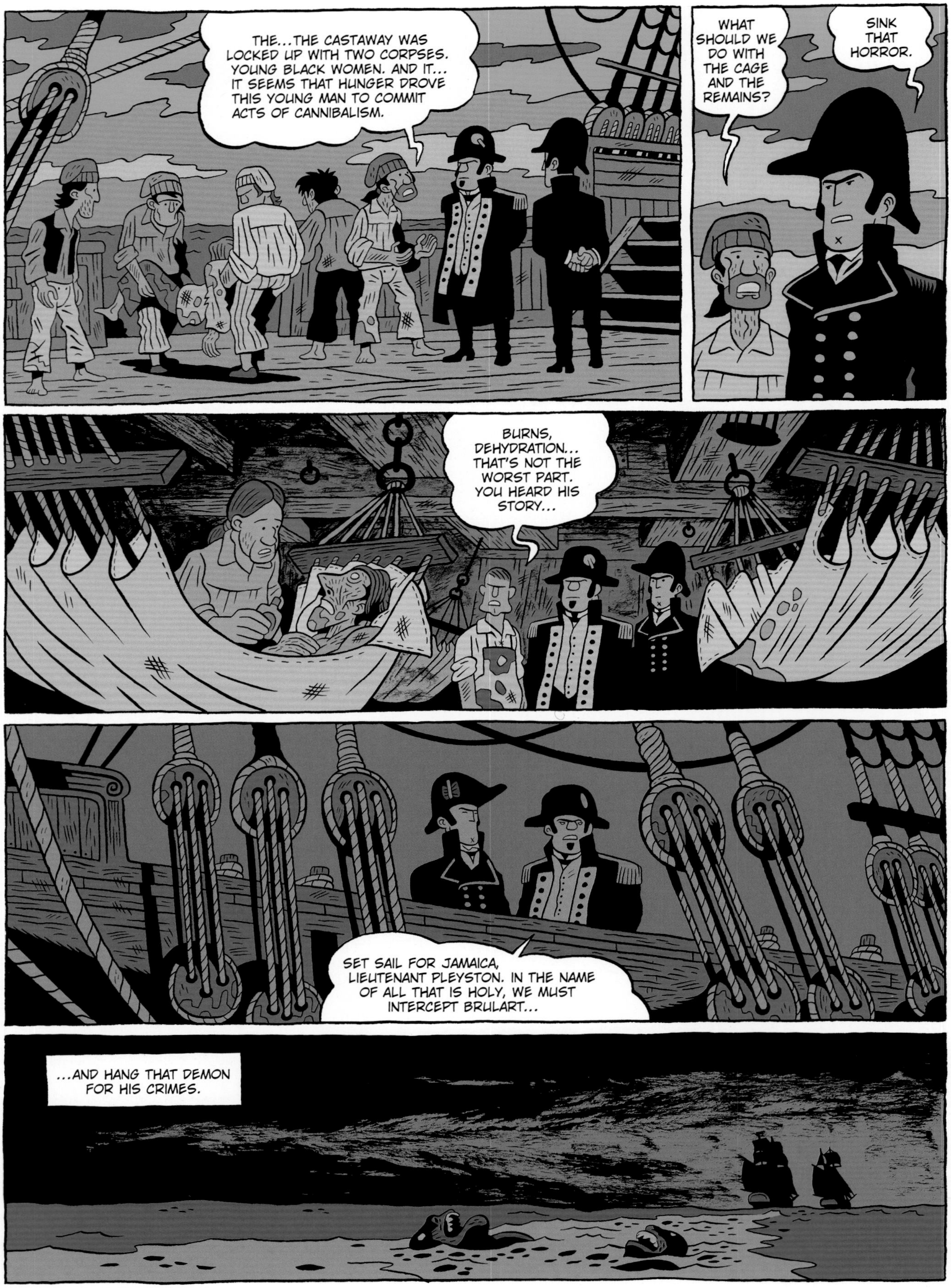

THE...THE CASTAWAY WAS LOCKED UP WITH TWO CORPSES. YOUNG BLACK WOMEN. AND IT... IT SEEMS THAT HUNGER DROVE THIS YOUNG MAN TO COMMIT ACTS OF CANNIBALISM.
WHAT SHOULD WE DO WITH THE CAGE AND THE REMAINS?
SINK THAT HORROR.
BURNS, DEHYDRATION... THAT'S NOT THE WORST PART. YOU HEARD HIS STORY...
SET SAIL FOR JAMAICA, LIEUTENANT PLEYSTON. IN THE NAME OF ALL THAT IS HOLY, WE MUST INTERCEPT BRULART...
...AND HANG THAT DEMON FOR HIS CRIMES.

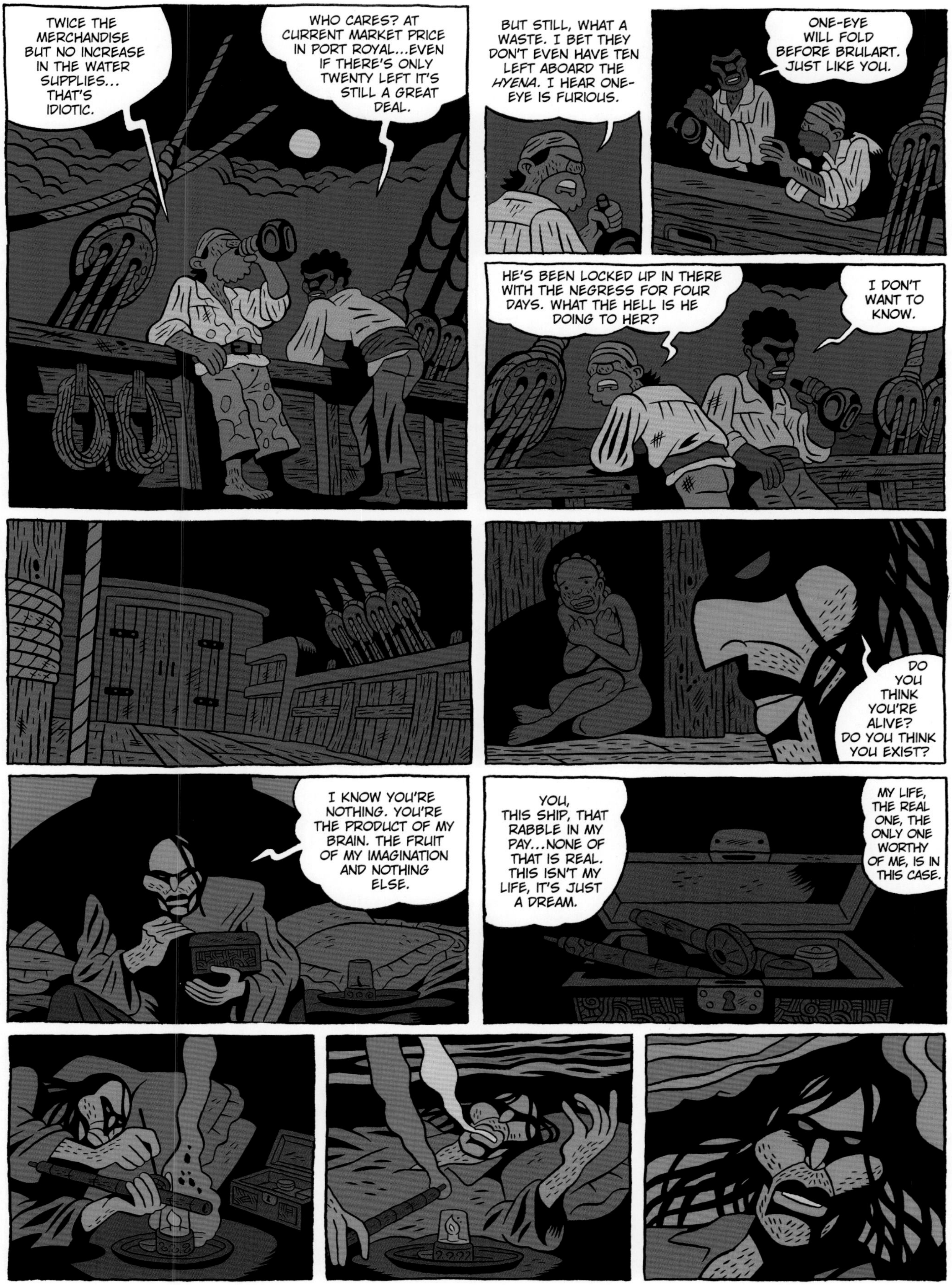
TWICE THE MERCHANDISE BUT NO INCREASE IN THE WATER SUPPLIES... THAT'S IDIOTIC.
WHO CARES? AT CURRENT MARKET PRICE IN PORT ROYAL...EVEN IF THERE'S ONLY TWENTY LEFT IT'S STILL A GREAT DEAL.
BUT STILL, WHAT A WASTE. I BET THEY DON'T EVEN HAVE TEN LEFT ABOARD THE *HYENA*. I HEAR ONE-EYE IS FURIOUS.
ONE-EYE WILL FOLD BEFORE BRULART. JUST LIKE YOU.
HE'S BEEN LOCKED UP IN THERE WITH THE NEGRESS FOR FOUR DAYS. WHAT THE HELL IS HE DOING TO HER?
I DON'T WANT TO KNOW.
DO YOU THINK YOU'RE ALIVE? DO YOU THINK YOU EXIST?
I KNOW YOU'RE NOTHING. YOU'RE THE PRODUCT OF MY BRAIN. THE FRUIT OF MY IMAGINATION AND NOTHING ELSE.
YOU, THIS SHIP, THAT RABBLE IN MY PAY...NONE OF THAT IS REAL. THIS ISN'T MY LIFE, IT'S JUST A DREAM.
MY LIFE, THE REAL ONE, THE ONLY ONE WORTHY OF ME, IS IN THIS CASE.

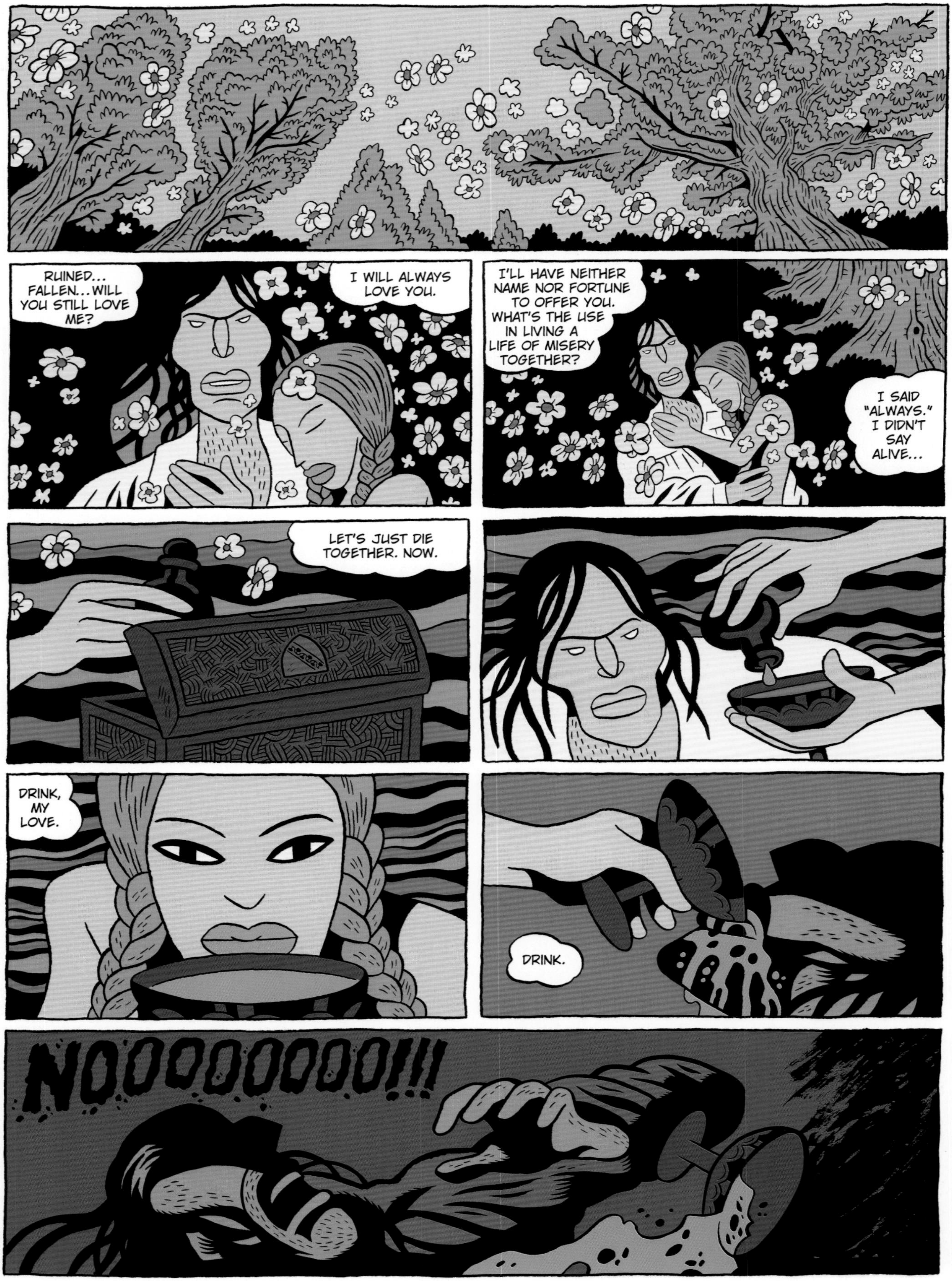
RUINED... FALLEN... WILL YOU STILL LOVE ME?
I WILL ALWAYS LOVE YOU.
I'LL HAVE NEITHER NAME NOR FORTUNE TO OFFER YOU. WHAT'S THE USE IN LIVING A LIFE OF MISERY TOGETHER?
I SAID "ALWAYS." I DIDN'T SAY ALIVE...
LET'S JUST DIE TOGETHER. NOW.
DRINK, MY LOVE.
DRINK.
NOOOOOOOO!!!

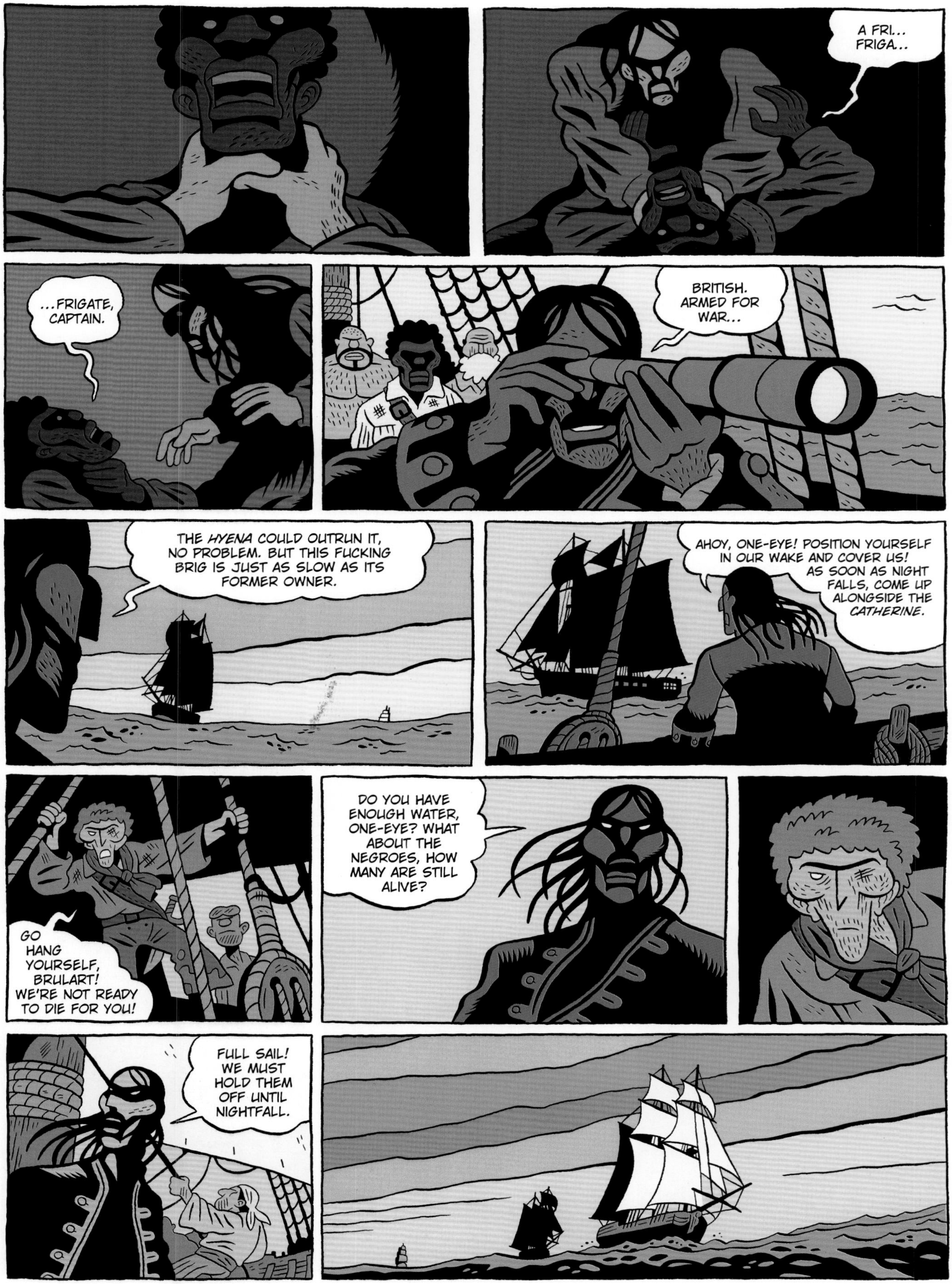
A FRI... FRIGA...
...FRIGATE, CAPTAIN.
BRITISH. ARMED FOR WAR...
THE *HYENA* COULD OUTRUN IT, NO PROBLEM. BUT THIS FUCKING BRIG IS JUST AS SLOW AS ITS FORMER OWNER.
AHOY, ONE-EYE! POSITION YOURSELF IN OUR WAKE AND COVER US! AS SOON AS NIGHT FALLS, COME UP ALONGSIDE THE *CATHERINE*.
GO HANG YOURSELF, BRULART! WE'RE NOT READY TO DIE FOR YOU!
DO YOU HAVE ENOUGH WATER, ONE-EYE? WHAT ABOUT THE NEGROES, HOW MANY ARE STILL ALIVE?
FULL SAIL! WE MUST HOLD THEM OFF UNTIL NIGHTFALL.

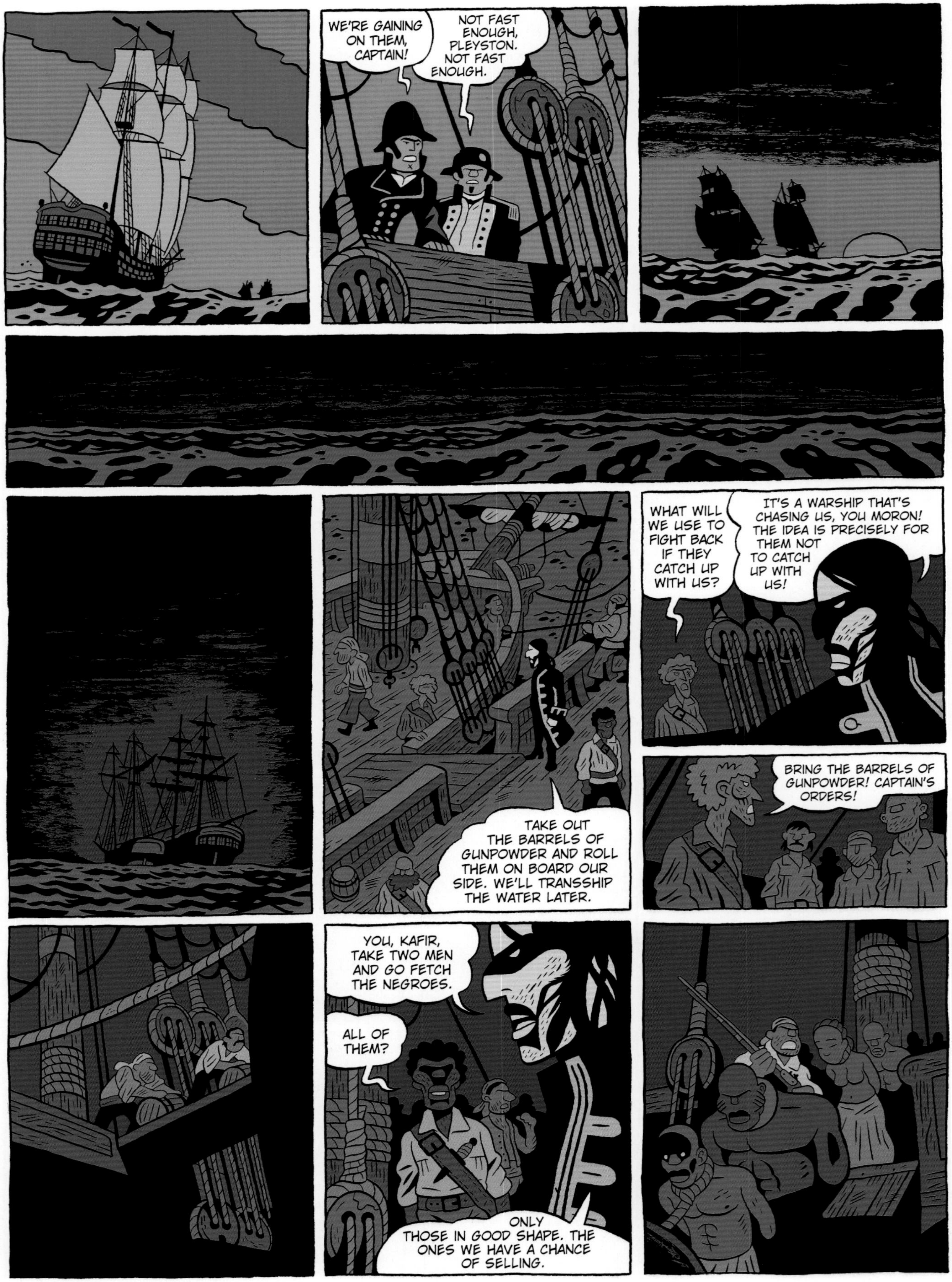
WE'RE GAINING ON THEM, CAPTAIN!
NOT FAST ENOUGH, PLEYSTON. NOT FAST ENOUGH.
TAKE OUT THE BARRELS OF GUNPOWDER AND ROLL THEM ON BOARD OUR SIDE. WE'LL TRANSSHIP THE WATER LATER.
WHAT WILL WE USE TO FIGHT BACK IF THEY CATCH UP WITH US?
IT'S A WARSHIP THAT'S CHASING US, YOU MORON! THE IDEA IS PRECISELY FOR THEM NOT TO CATCH UP WITH US!
BRING THE BARRELS OF GUNPOWDER! CAPTAIN'S ORDERS!
YOU, KAFIR, TAKE TWO MEN AND GO FETCH THE NEGROES.
ALL OF THEM?
ONLY THOSE IN GOOD SHAPE. THE ONES WE HAVE A CHANCE OF SELLING.

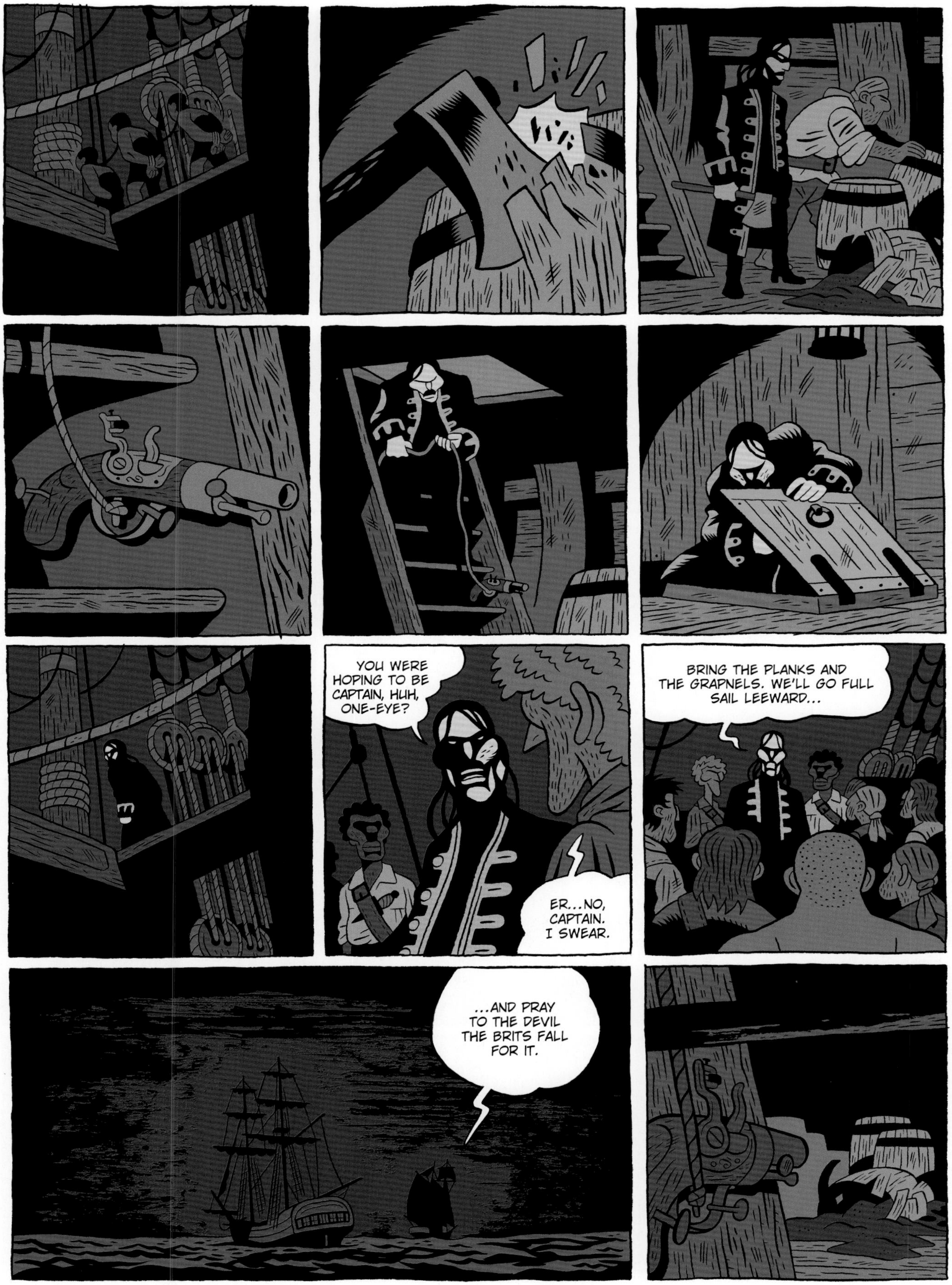
YOU WERE HOPING TO BE CAPTAIN, HUH, ONE-EYE?
ER...NO, CAPTAIN. I SWEAR.
BRING THE PLANKS AND THE GRAPNELS. WE'LL GO FULL SAIL LEEWARD...
...AND PRAY TO THE DEVIL THE BRITS FALL FOR IT.

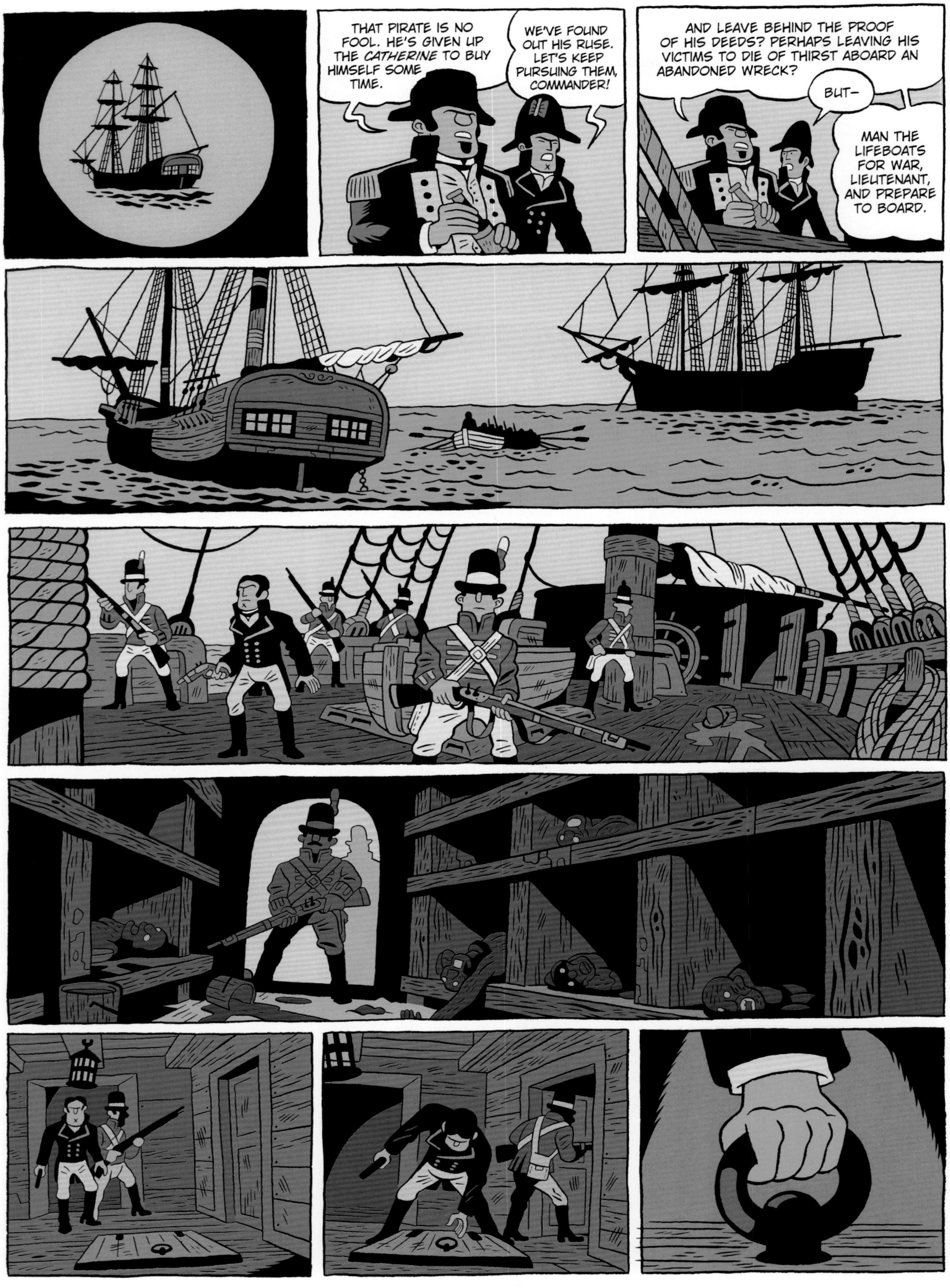
THAT PIRATE IS NO FOOL. HE'S GIVEN UP THE *CATHERINE* TO BUY HIMSELF SOME TIME.
WE'VE FOUND OUT HIS RUSE. LET'S KEEP PURSUING THEM, COMMANDER!
AND LEAVE BEHIND THE PROOF OF HIS DEEDS? PERHAPS LEAVING HIS VICTIMS TO DIE OF THIRST ABOARD AN ABANDONED WRECK?
BUT–
MAN THE LIFEBOATS FOR WAR, LIEUTENANT, AND PREPARE TO BOARD.

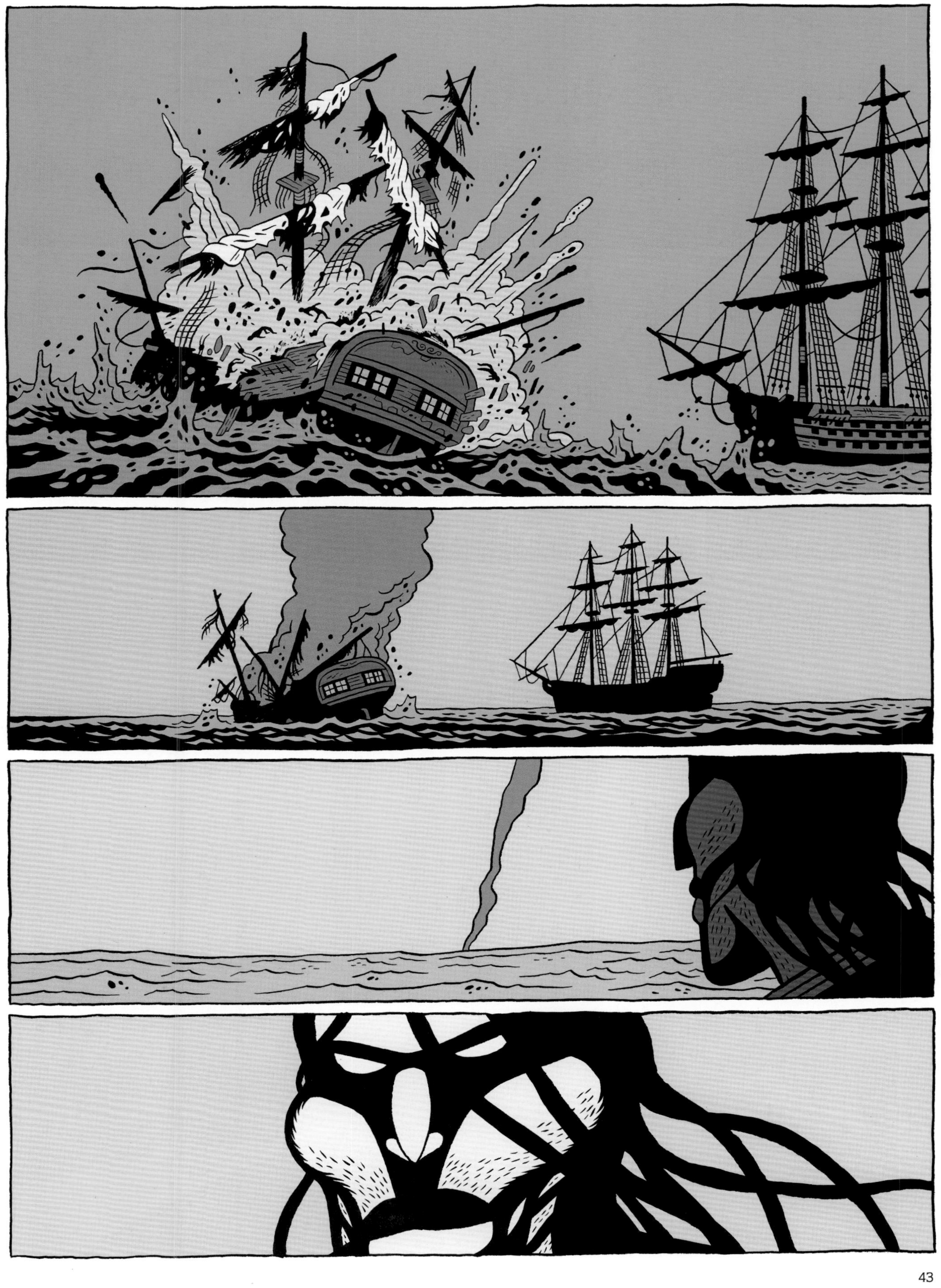

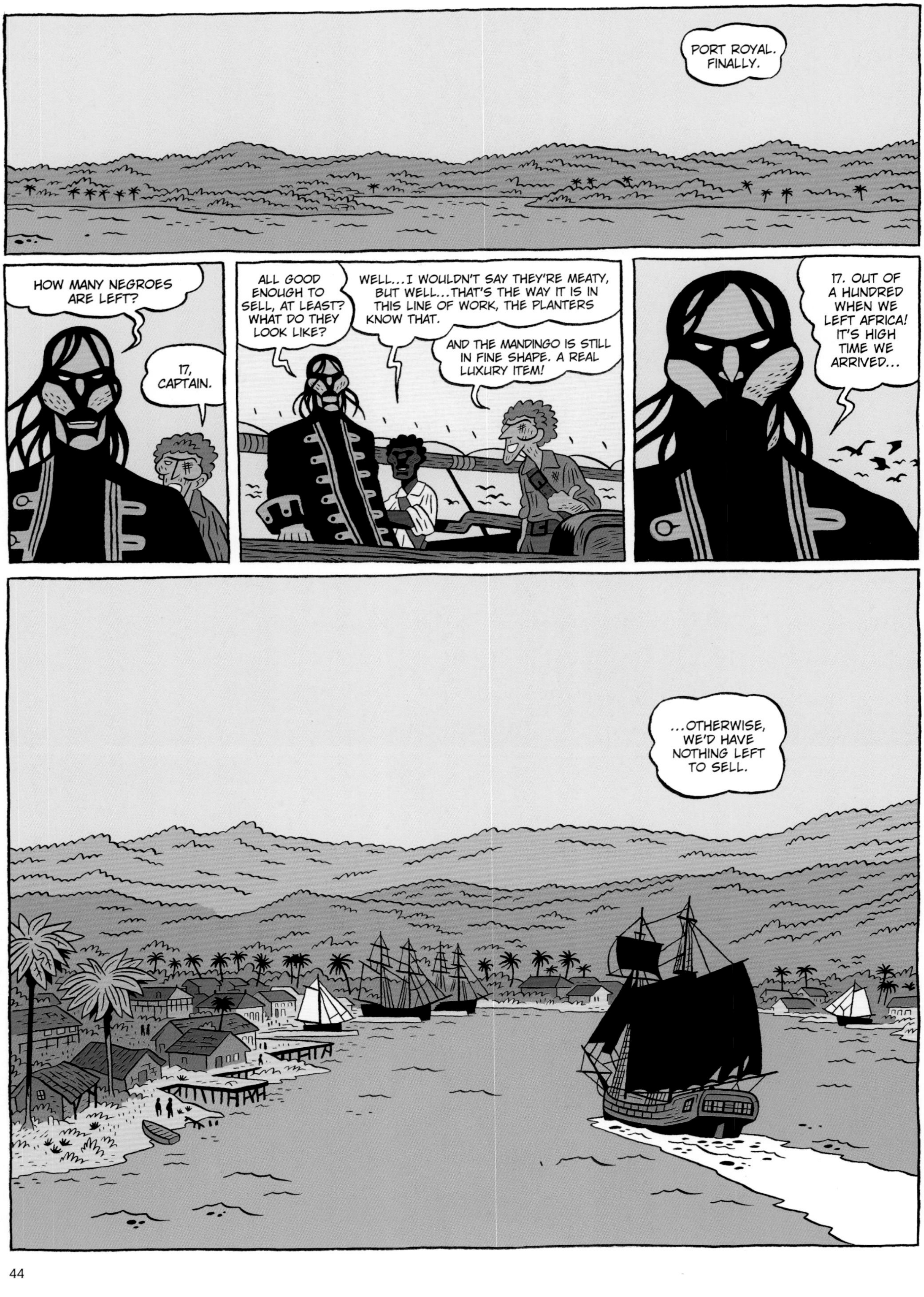
PORT ROYAL. FINALLY.
HOW MANY NEGROES ARE LEFT?
17, CAPTAIN.
ALL GOOD ENOUGH TO SELL, AT LEAST? WHAT DO THEY LOOK LIKE?
WELL... I WOULDN'T SAY THEY'RE MEATY, BUT WELL... THAT'S THE WAY IT IS IN THIS LINE OF WORK, THE PLANTERS KNOW THAT.
AND THE MANDINGO IS STILL IN FINE SHAPE. A REAL LUXURY ITEM!
17. OUT OF A HUNDRED WHEN WE LEFT AFRICA! IT'S HIGH TIME WE ARRIVED...
...OTHERWISE, WE'D HAVE NOTHING LEFT TO SELL.

BOOK II

The Plantation

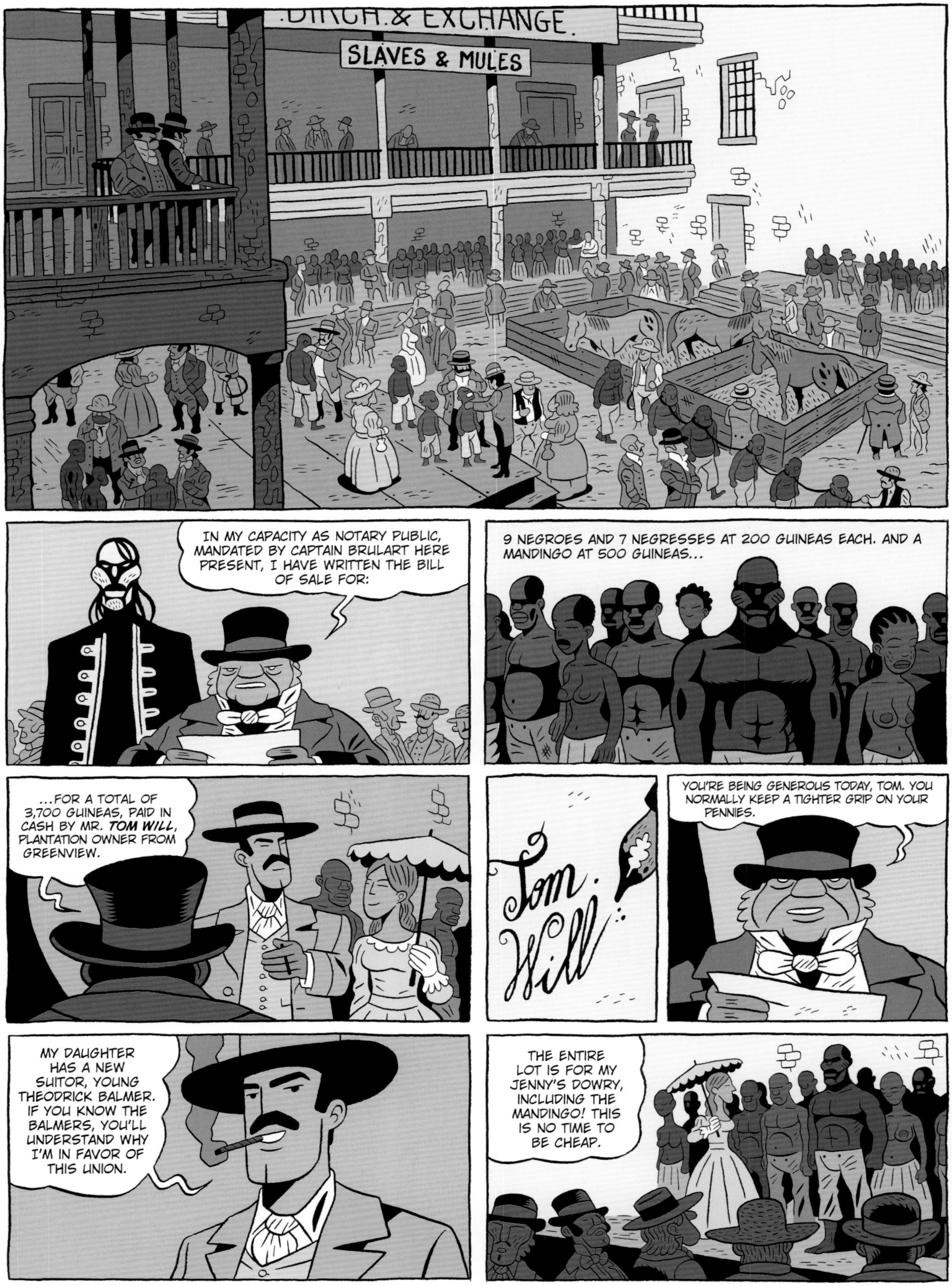
.DIRCH.& EXCHANGE.
SLAVES & MULES
IN MY CAPACITY AS NOTARY PUBLIC, MANDATED BY CAPTAIN BRULART HERE PRESENT, I HAVE WRITTEN THE BILL OF SALE FOR:
9 NEGROES AND 7 NEGRESSES AT 200 GUINEAS EACH. AND A MANDINGO AT 500 GUINEAS...
...FOR A TOTAL OF 3,700 GUINEAS, PAID IN CASH BY MR. TOM WILL, PLANTATION OWNER FROM GREENVIEW.
Tom Will
YOU'RE BEING GENEROUS TODAY, TOM. YOU NORMALLY KEEP A TIGHTER GRIP ON YOUR PENNIES.
MY DAUGHTER HAS A NEW SUITOR, YOUNG THEODRICK BALMER. IF YOU KNOW THE BALMERS, YOU'LL UNDERSTAND WHY I'M IN FAVOR OF THIS UNION.
THE ENTIRE LOT IS FOR MY JENNY'S DOWRY, INCLUDING THE MANDINGO! THIS IS NO TIME TO BE CHEAP.

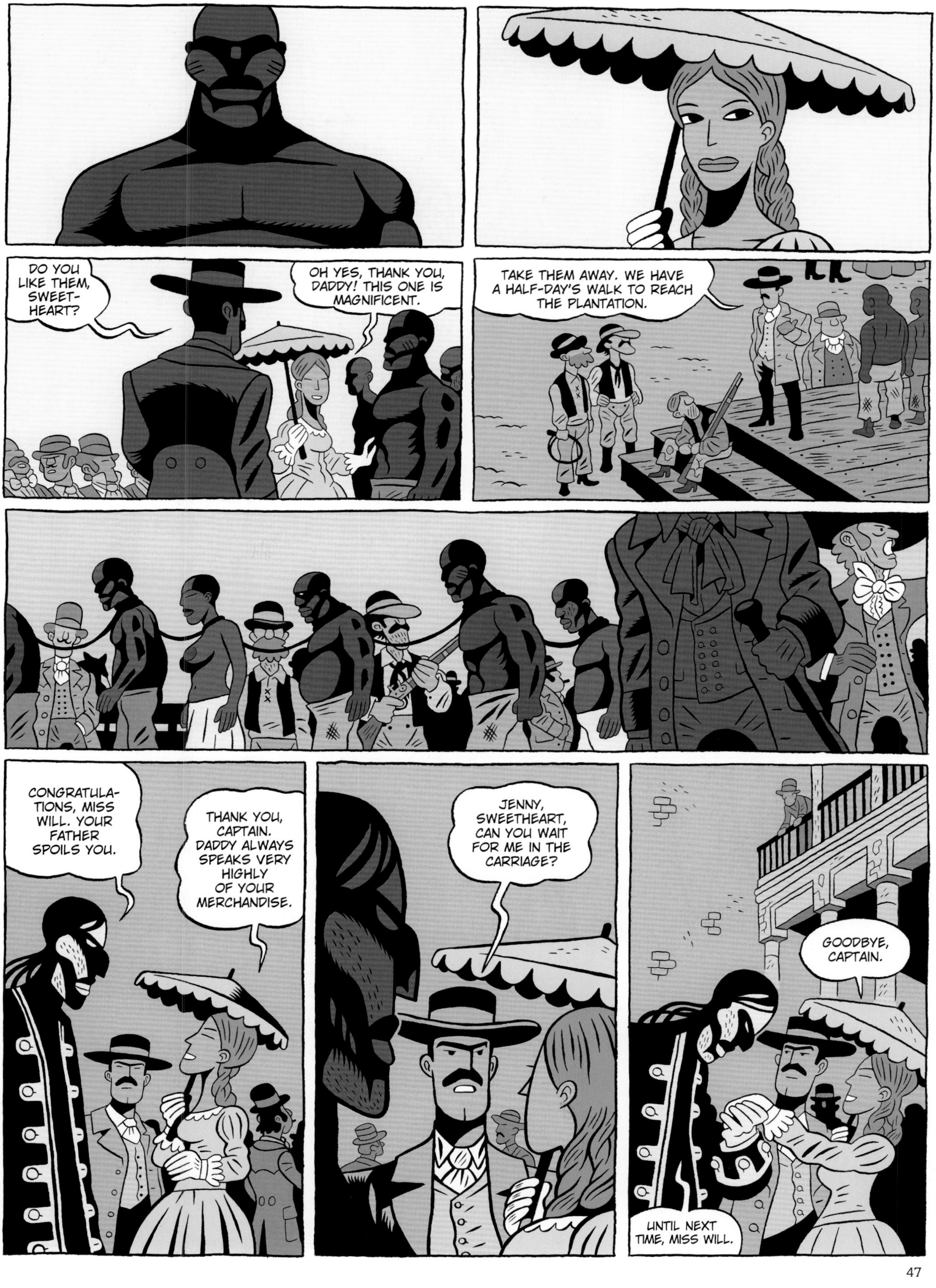

DO YOU LIKE THEM, SWEET-HEART?
OH YES, THANK YOU, DADDY! THIS ONE IS MAGNIFICENT.
TAKE THEM AWAY. WE HAVE A HALF-DAY'S WALK TO REACH THE PLANTATION.
CONGRATULA-TIONS, MISS WILL. YOUR FATHER SPOILS YOU.
THANK YOU, CAPTAIN. DADDY ALWAYS SPEAKS VERY HIGHLY OF YOUR MERCHANDISE.
JENNY, SWEETHEART, CAN YOU WAIT FOR ME IN THE CARRIAGE?
GOODBYE, CAPTAIN.
UNTIL NEXT TIME, MISS WILL.

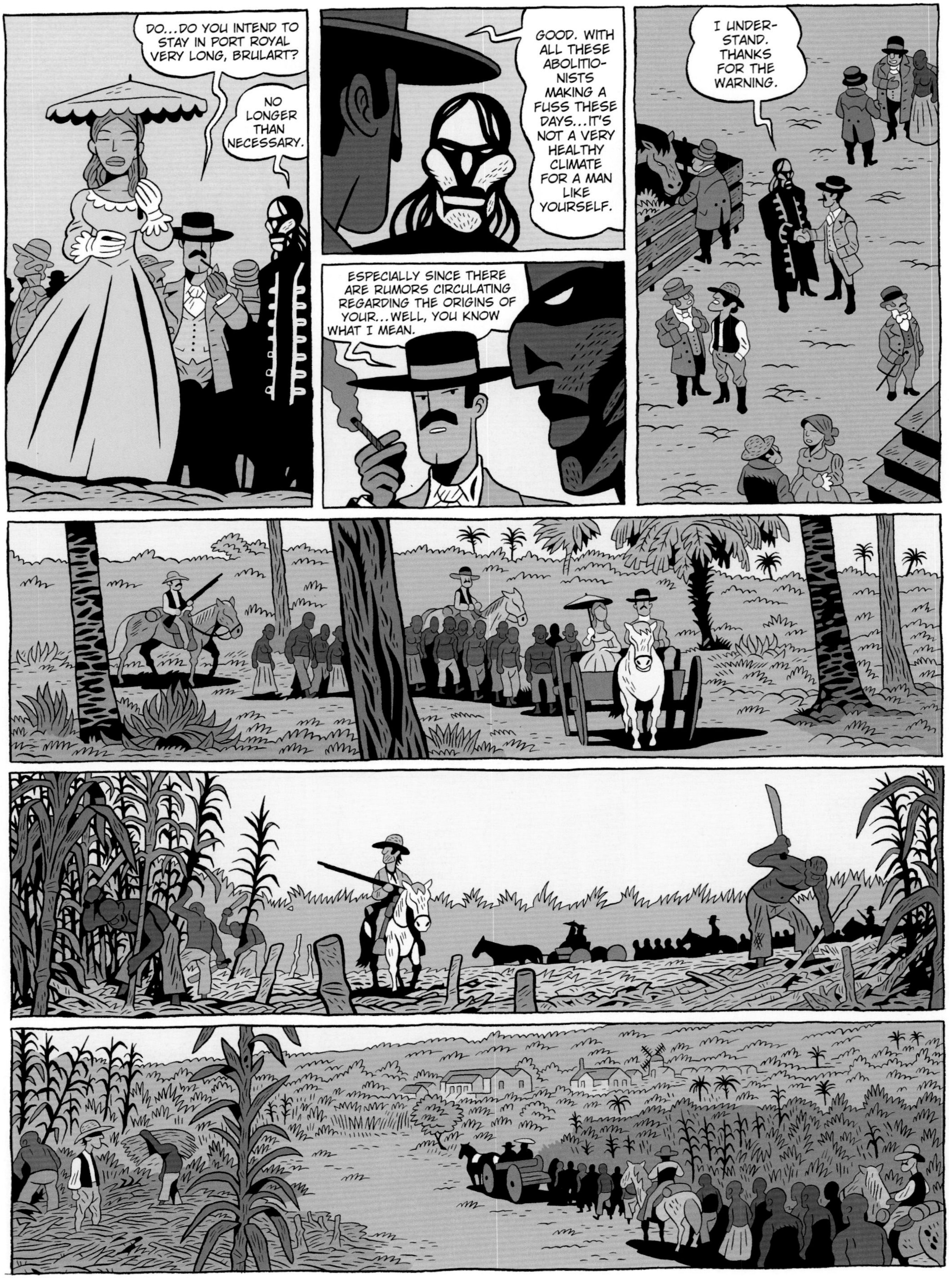
DO...DO YOU INTEND TO STAY IN PORT ROYAL VERY LONG, BRULART?
NO LONGER THAN NECESSARY.
GOOD. WITH ALL THESE ABOLITIONISTS MAKING A FUSS THESE DAYS...IT'S NOT A VERY HEALTHY CLIMATE FOR A MAN LIKE YOURSELF.
ESPECIALLY SINCE THERE ARE RUMORS CIRCULATING REGARDING THE ORIGINS OF YOUR...WELL, YOU KNOW WHAT I MEAN.
I UNDERSTAND. THANKS FOR THE WARNING.

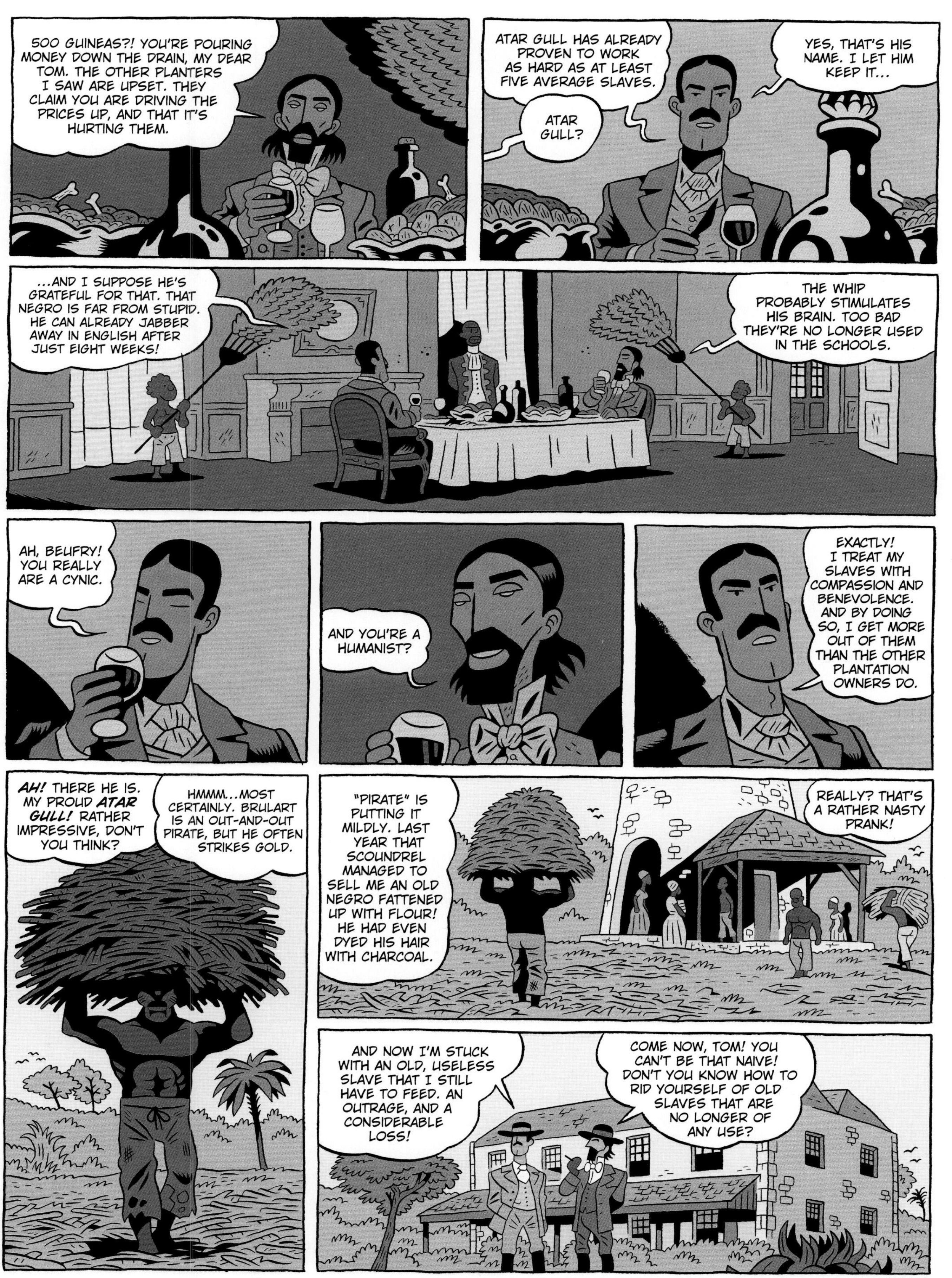
500 GUINEAS?! YOU'RE POURING MONEY DOWN THE DRAIN, MY DEAR TOM. THE OTHER PLANTERS I SAW ARE UPSET. THEY CLAIM YOU ARE DRIVING THE PRICES UP, AND THAT IT'S HURTING THEM.
ATAR GULL HAS ALREADY PROVEN TO WORK AS HARD AS AT LEAST FIVE AVERAGE SLAVES.
ATAR GULL?
YES, THAT'S HIS NAME. I LET HIM KEEP IT...
...AND I SUPPOSE HE'S GRATEFUL FOR THAT. THAT NEGRO IS FAR FROM STUPID. HE CAN ALREADY JABBER AWAY IN ENGLISH AFTER JUST EIGHT WEEKS!
THE WHIP PROBABLY STIMULATES HIS BRAIN. TOO BAD THEY'RE NO LONGER USED IN THE SCHOOLS.
AH, BEUFRY! YOU REALLY ARE A CYNIC.
AND YOU'RE A HUMANIST?
EXACTLY! I TREAT MY SLAVES WITH COMPASSION AND BENEVOLENCE. AND BY DOING SO, I GET MORE OUT OF THEM THAN THE OTHER PLANTATION OWNERS DO.
AH! THERE HE IS. MY PROUD ATAR GULL! RATHER IMPRESSIVE, DON'T YOU THINK?
HMMM...MOST CERTAINLY. BRULART IS AN OUT-AND-OUT PIRATE, BUT HE OFTEN STRIKES GOLD.
"PIRATE" IS PUTTING IT MILDLY. LAST YEAR THAT SCOUNDREL MANAGED TO SELL ME AN OLD NEGRO FATTENED UP WITH FLOUR! HE HAD EVEN DYED HIS HAIR WITH CHARCOAL.
REALLY? THAT'S A RATHER NASTY PRANK!
AND NOW I'M STUCK WITH AN OLD, USELESS SLAVE THAT I STILL HAVE TO FEED. AN OUTRAGE, AND A CONSIDERABLE LOSS!
COME NOW, TOM! YOU CAN'T BE THAT NAIVE! DON'T YOU KNOW HOW TO RID YOURSELF OF OLD SLAVES THAT ARE NO LONGER OF ANY USE?

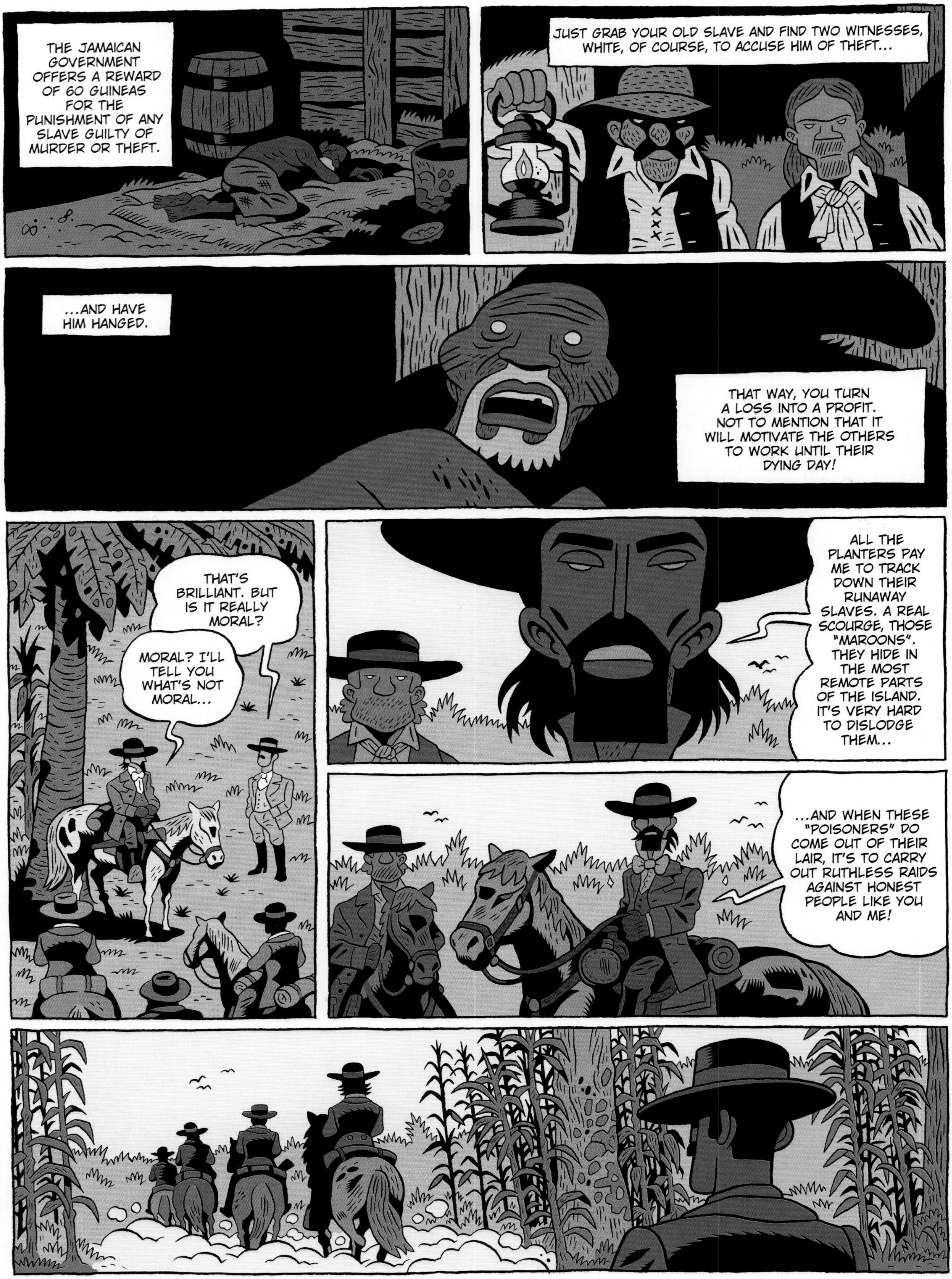
THE JAMAICAN GOVERNMENT OFFERS A REWARD OF 60 GUINEAS FOR THE PUNISHMENT OF ANY SLAVE GUILTY OF MURDER OR THEFT.
JUST GRAB YOUR OLD SLAVE AND FIND TWO WITNESSES, WHITE, OF COURSE, TO ACCUSE HIM OF THEFT...
...AND HAVE HIM HANGED.
THAT WAY, YOU TURN A LOSS INTO A PROFIT. NOT TO MENTION THAT IT WILL MOTIVATE THE OTHERS TO WORK UNTIL THEIR DYING DAY!
THAT'S BRILLIANT. BUT IS IT REALLY MORAL?
MORAL? I'LL TELL YOU WHAT'S NOT MORAL...
ALL THE PLANTERS PAY ME TO TRACK DOWN THEIR RUNAWAY SLAVES. A REAL SCOURGE, THOSE "MAROONS". THEY HIDE IN THE MOST REMOTE PARTS OF THE ISLAND. IT'S VERY HARD TO DISLODGE THEM...
...AND WHEN THESE "POISONERS" DO COME OUT OF THEIR LAIR, IT'S TO CARRY OUT RUTHLESS RAIDS AGAINST HONEST PEOPLE LIKE YOU AND ME!

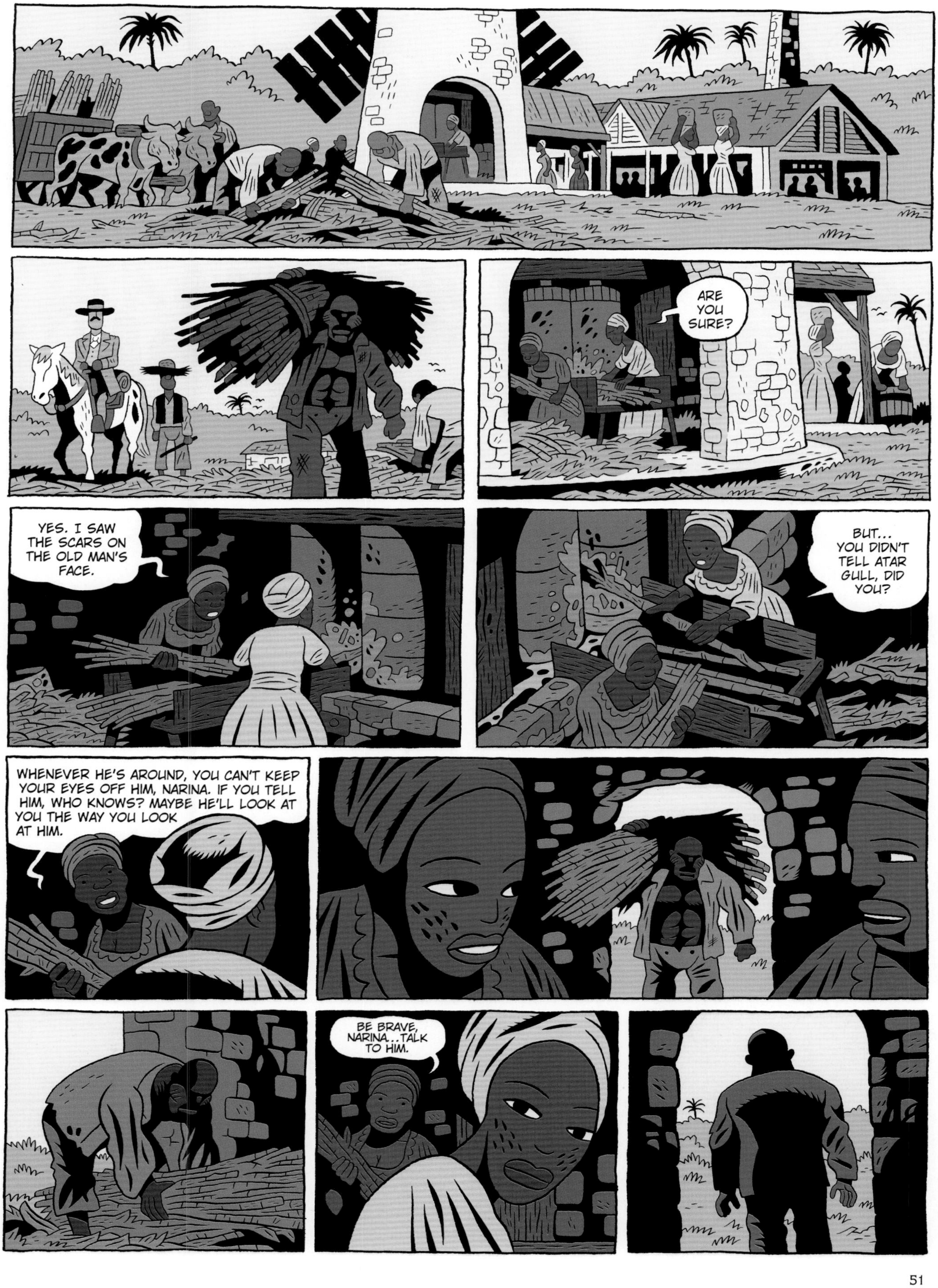
ARE YOU SURE?
YES. I SAW THE SCARS ON THE OLD MAN'S FACE.
BUT... YOU DIDN'T TELL ATAR GULL, DID YOU?
WHENEVER HE'S AROUND, YOU CAN'T KEEP YOUR EYES OFF HIM, NARINA. IF YOU TELL HIM, WHO KNOWS? MAYBE HE'LL LOOK AT YOU THE WAY YOU LOOK AT HIM.
BE BRAVE, NARINA...TALK TO HIM.

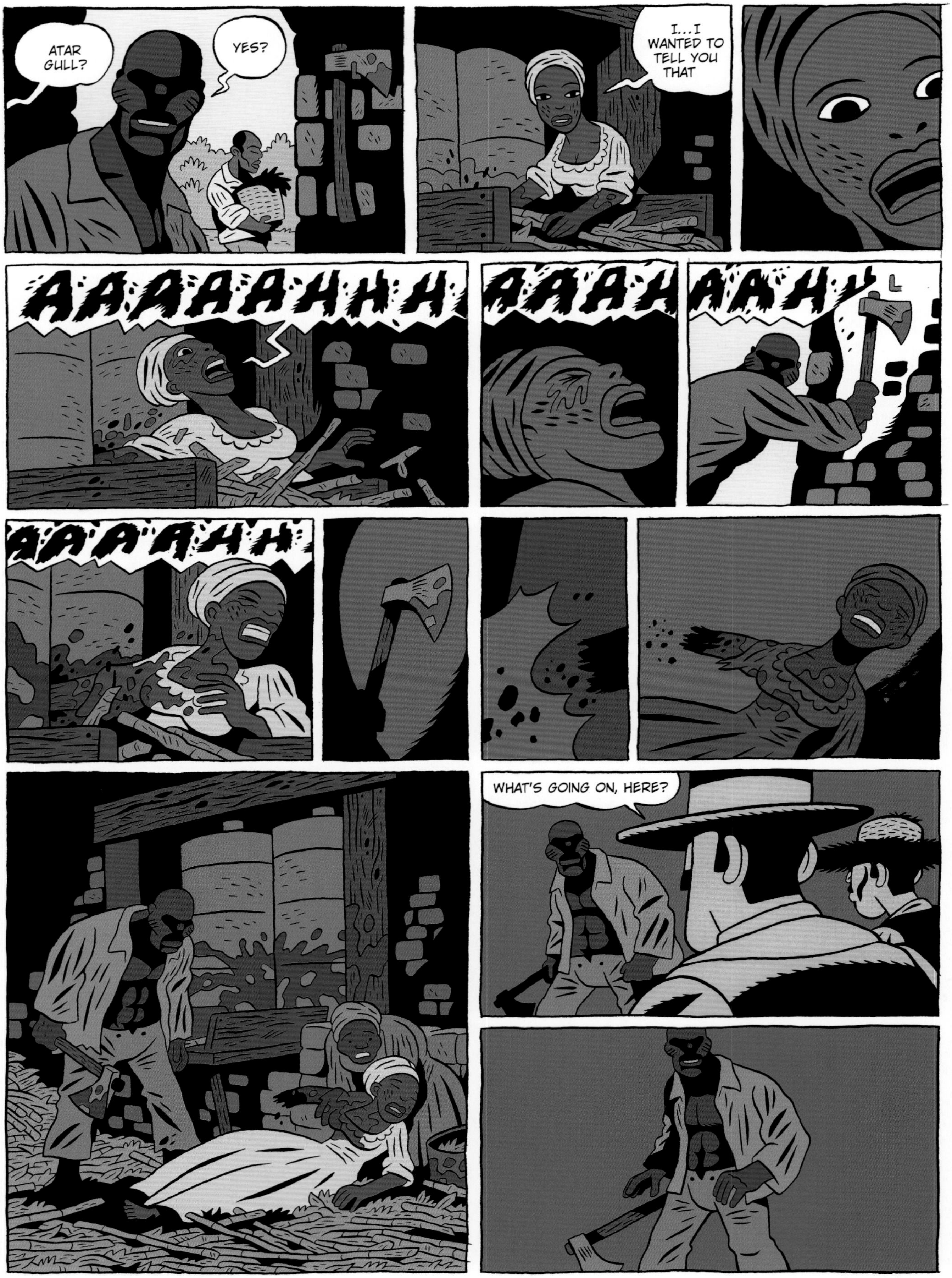
ATAR GULL?
YES?
I...I WANTED TO TELL YOU THAT
AAAAAAHHH
AAAAHAAAH
AAAAAHH
WHAT'S GOING ON, HERE?

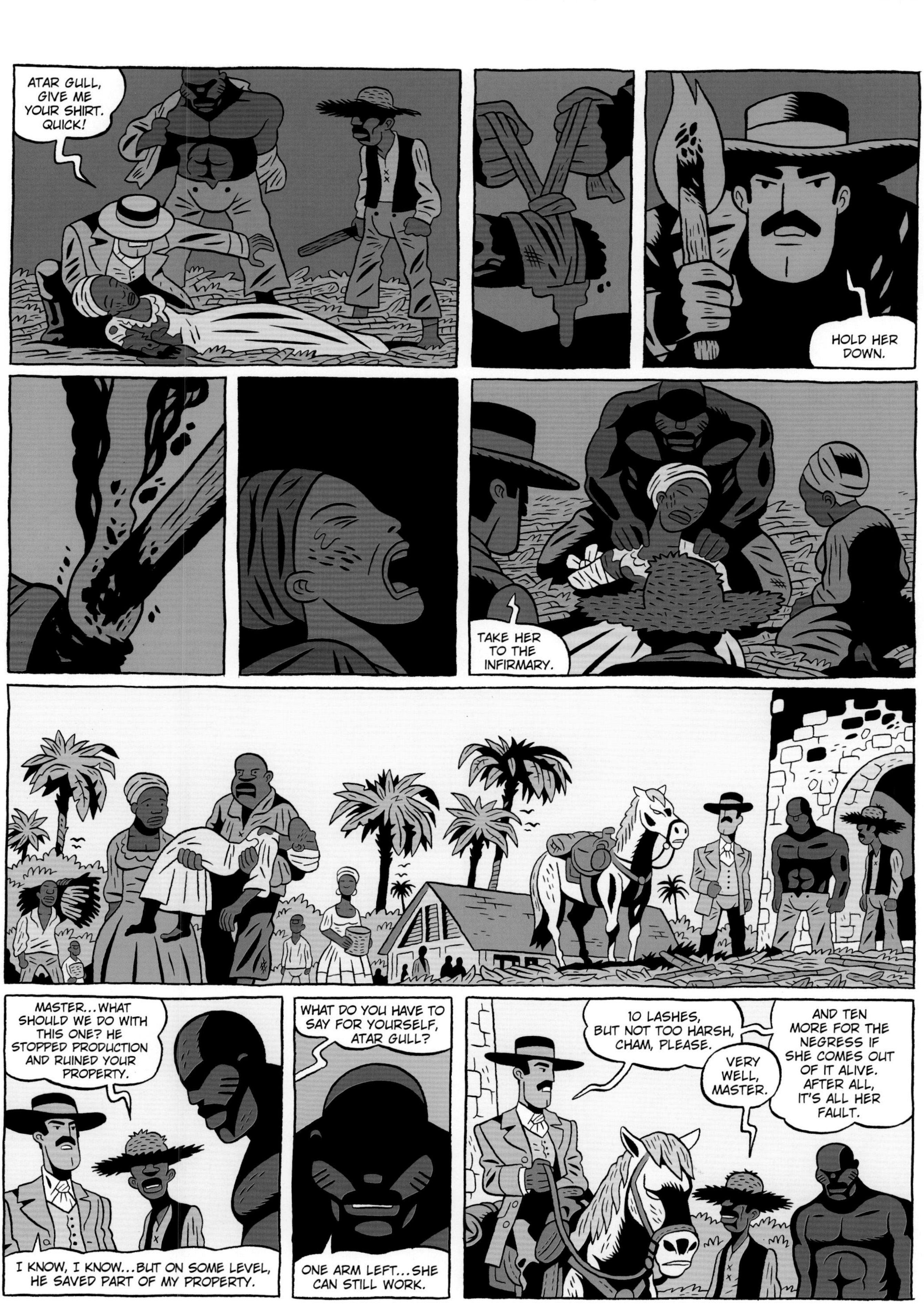
ATAR GULL, GIVE ME YOUR SHIRT. QUICK!
HOLD HER DOWN.
TAKE HER TO THE INFIRMARY.
MASTER...WHAT SHOULD WE DO WITH THIS ONE? HE STOPPED PRODUCTION AND RUINED YOUR PROPERTY.
I KNOW, I KNOW...BUT ON SOME LEVEL, HE SAVED PART OF MY PROPERTY.
WHAT DO YOU HAVE TO SAY FOR YOURSELF, ATAR GULL?
ONE ARM LEFT...SHE CAN STILL WORK.
10 LASHES, BUT NOT TOO HARSH, CHAM, PLEASE.
VERY WELL, MASTER.
AND TEN MORE FOR THE NEGRESS IF SHE COMES OUT OF IT ALIVE. AFTER ALL, IT'S ALL HER FAULT.

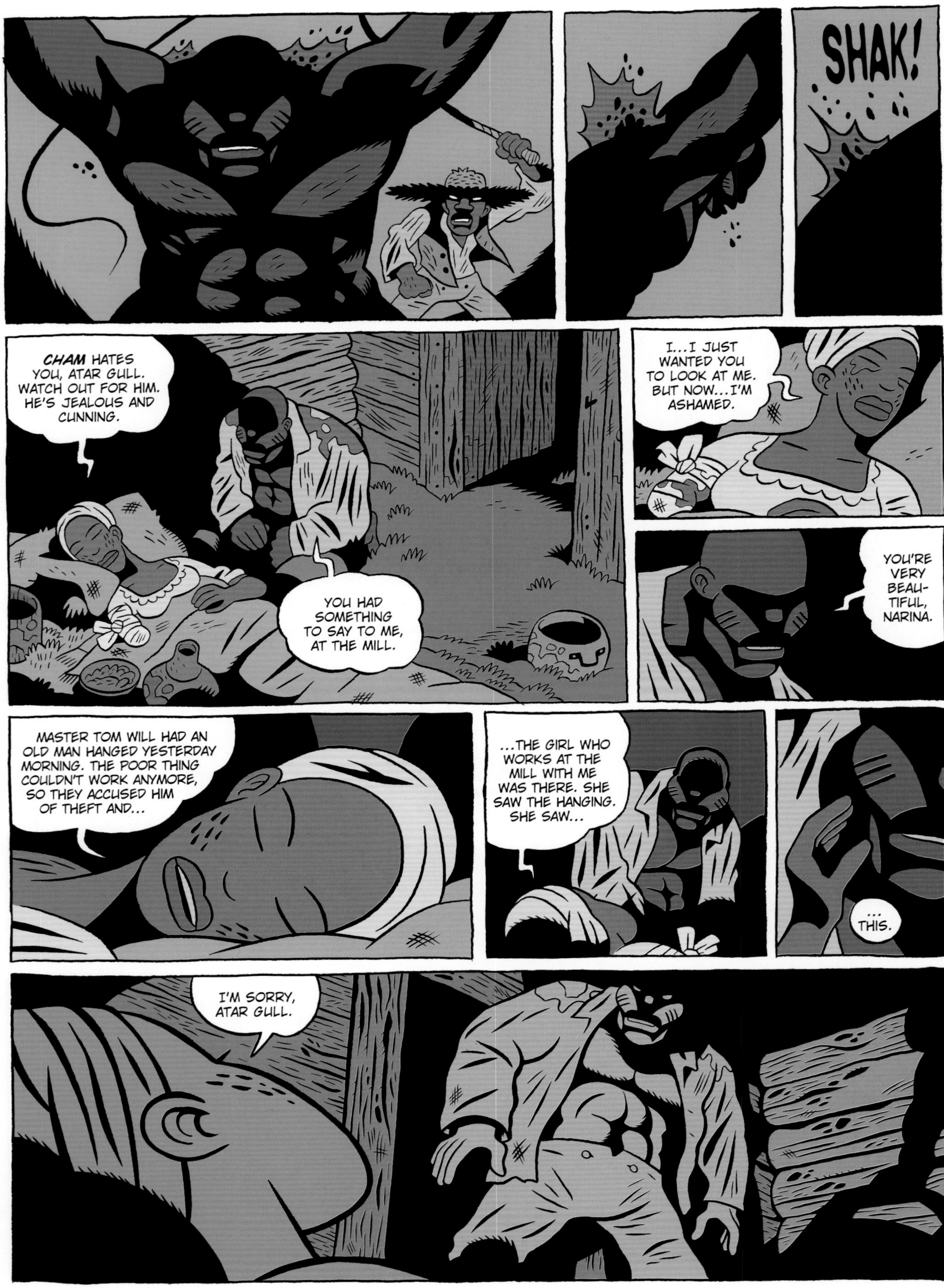
SHAK!
CHAM HATES YOU, ATAR GULL. WATCH OUT FOR HIM. HE'S JEALOUS AND CUNNING.
YOU HAD SOMETHING TO SAY TO ME, AT THE MILL.
I...I JUST WANTED YOU TO LOOK AT ME. BUT NOW...I'M ASHAMED.
YOU'RE VERY BEAUTIFUL, NARINA.
MASTER TOM WILL HAD AN OLD MAN HANGED YESTERDAY MORNING. THE POOR THING COULDN'T WORK ANYMORE, SO THEY ACCUSED HIM OF THEFT AND...
...THE GIRL WHO WORKS AT THE MILL WITH ME WAS THERE. SHE SAW THE HANGING. SHE SAW...
...THIS.
I'M SORRY, ATAR GULL.

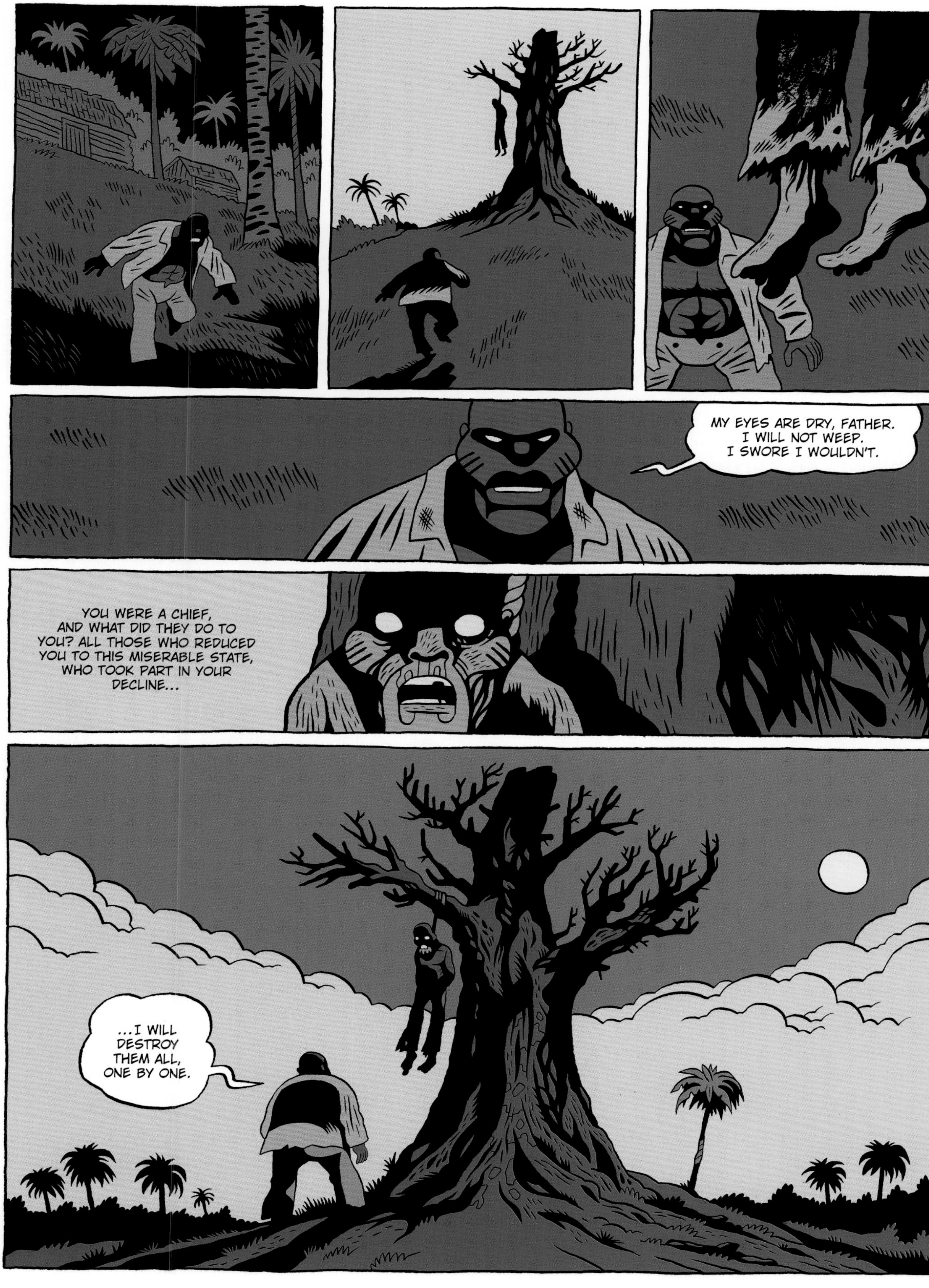
MY EYES ARE DRY, FATHER. I WILL NOT WEEP. I SWORE I WOULDN'T.
YOU WERE A CHIEF, AND WHAT DID THEY DO TO YOU? ALL THOSE WHO REDUCED YOU TO THIS MISERABLE STATE, WHO TOOK PART IN YOUR DECLINE...
...I WILL DESTROY THEM ALL, ONE BY ONE.

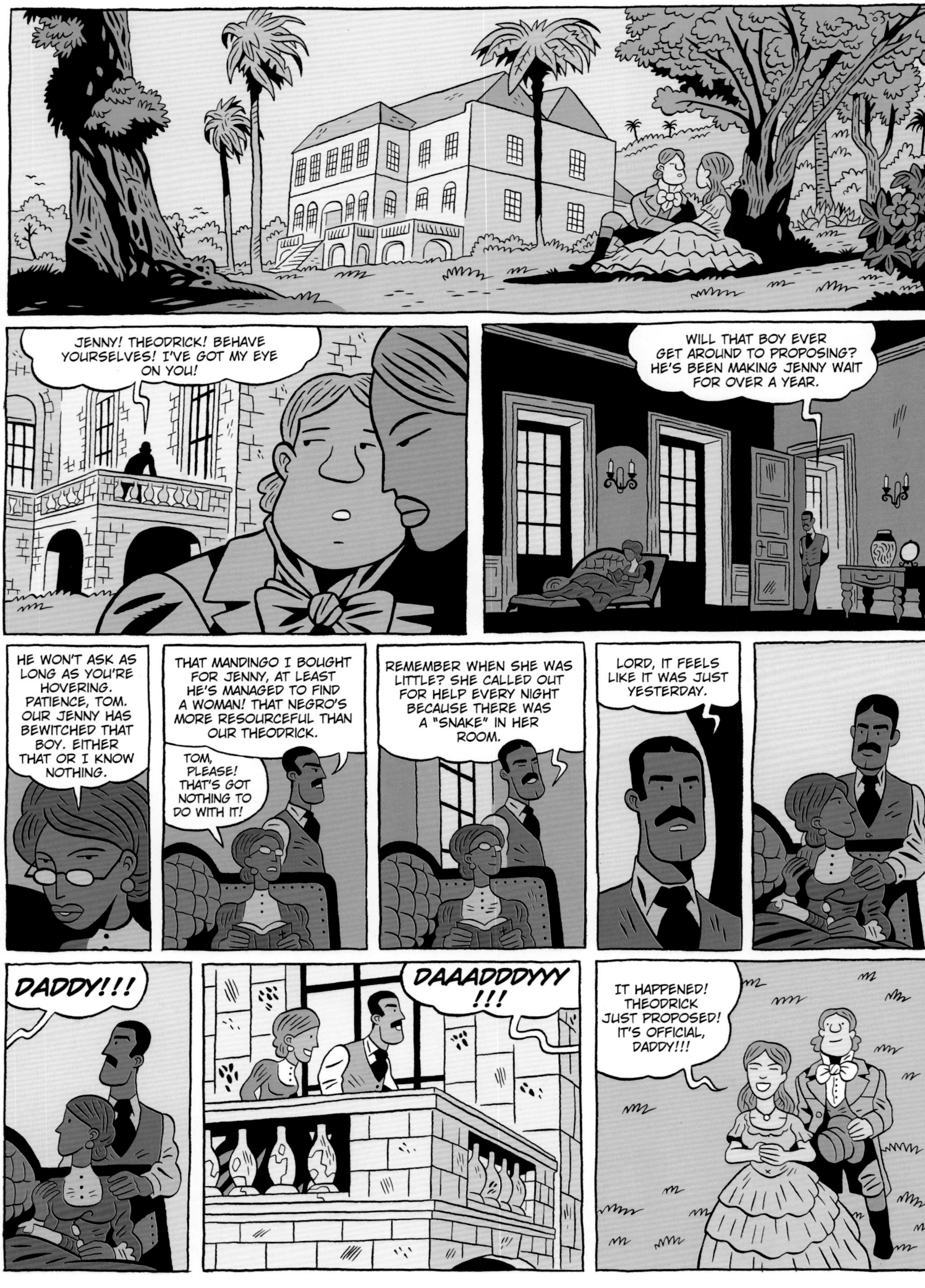
JENNY! THEODRICK! BEHAVE YOURSELVES! I'VE GOT MY EYE ON YOU!
WILL THAT BOY EVER GET AROUND TO PROPOSING? HE'S BEEN MAKING JENNY WAIT FOR OVER A YEAR.
HE WON'T ASK AS LONG AS YOU'RE HOVERING. PATIENCE, TOM. OUR JENNY HAS BEWITCHED THAT BOY. EITHER THAT OR I KNOW NOTHING.
THAT MANDINGO I BOUGHT FOR JENNY, AT LEAST HE'S MANAGED TO FIND A WOMAN! THAT NEGRO'S MORE RESOURCEFUL THAN OUR THEODRICK.
TOM, PLEASE! THAT'S GOT NOTHING TO DO WITH IT!
REMEMBER WHEN SHE WAS LITTLE? SHE CALLED OUT FOR HELP EVERY NIGHT BECAUSE THERE WAS A "SNAKE" IN HER ROOM.
LORD, IT FEELS LIKE IT WAS JUST YESTERDAY.
DADDY!!!
DAAADDDYYY !!!
IT HAPPENED! THEODRICK JUST PROPOSED! IT'S OFFICIAL, DADDY!!!

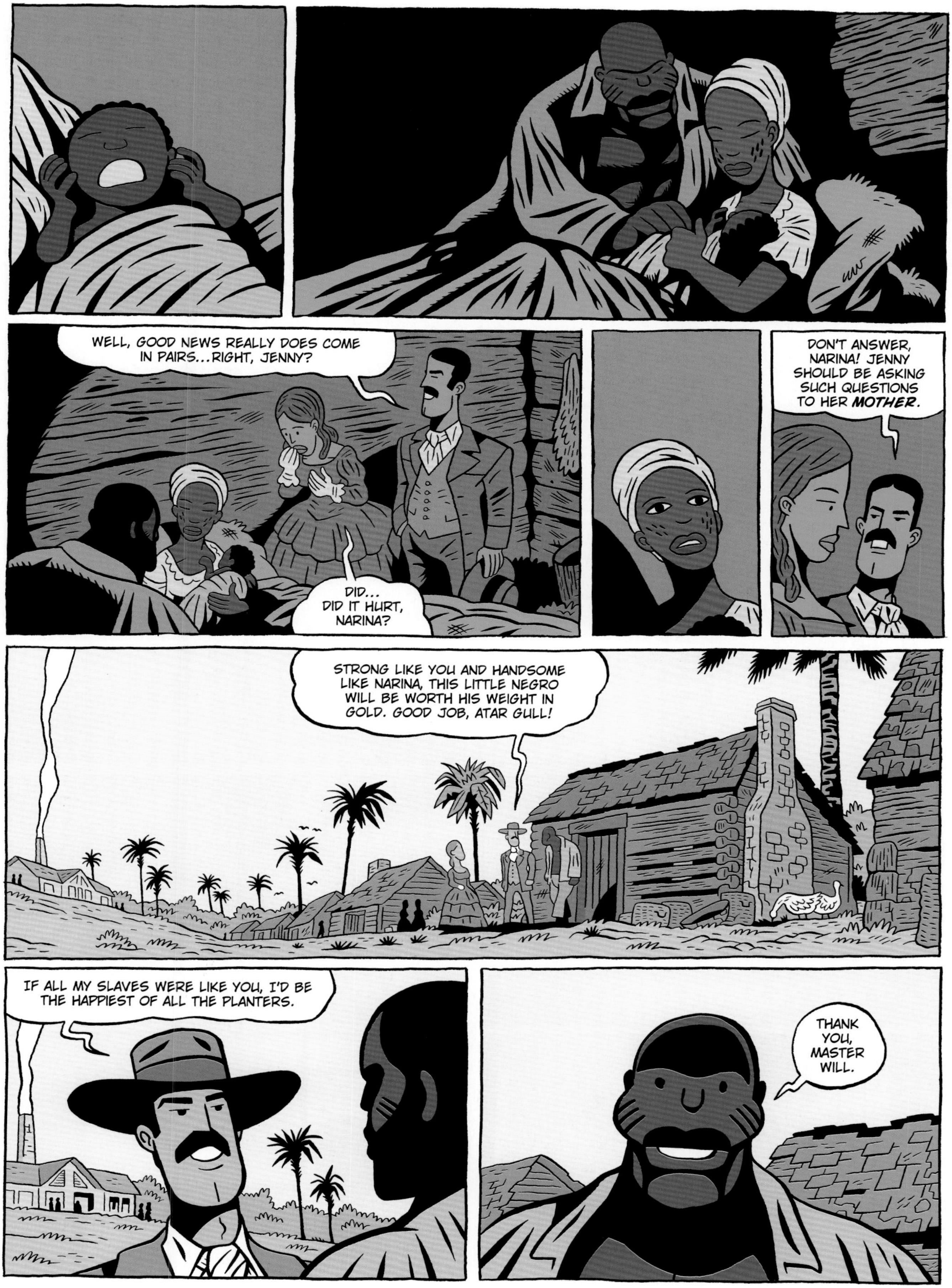
WELL, GOOD NEWS REALLY DOES COME IN PAIRS... RIGHT, JENNY?
DID... DID IT HURT, NARINA?
DON'T ANSWER, NARINA! JENNY SHOULD BE ASKING SUCH QUESTIONS TO HER ***MOTHER***.
STRONG LIKE YOU AND HANDSOME LIKE NARINA, THIS LITTLE NEGRO WILL BE WORTH HIS WEIGHT IN GOLD. GOOD JOB, ATAR GULL!
IF ALL MY SLAVES WERE LIKE YOU, I'D BE THE HAPPIEST OF ALL THE PLANTERS.
THANK YOU, MASTER WILL.

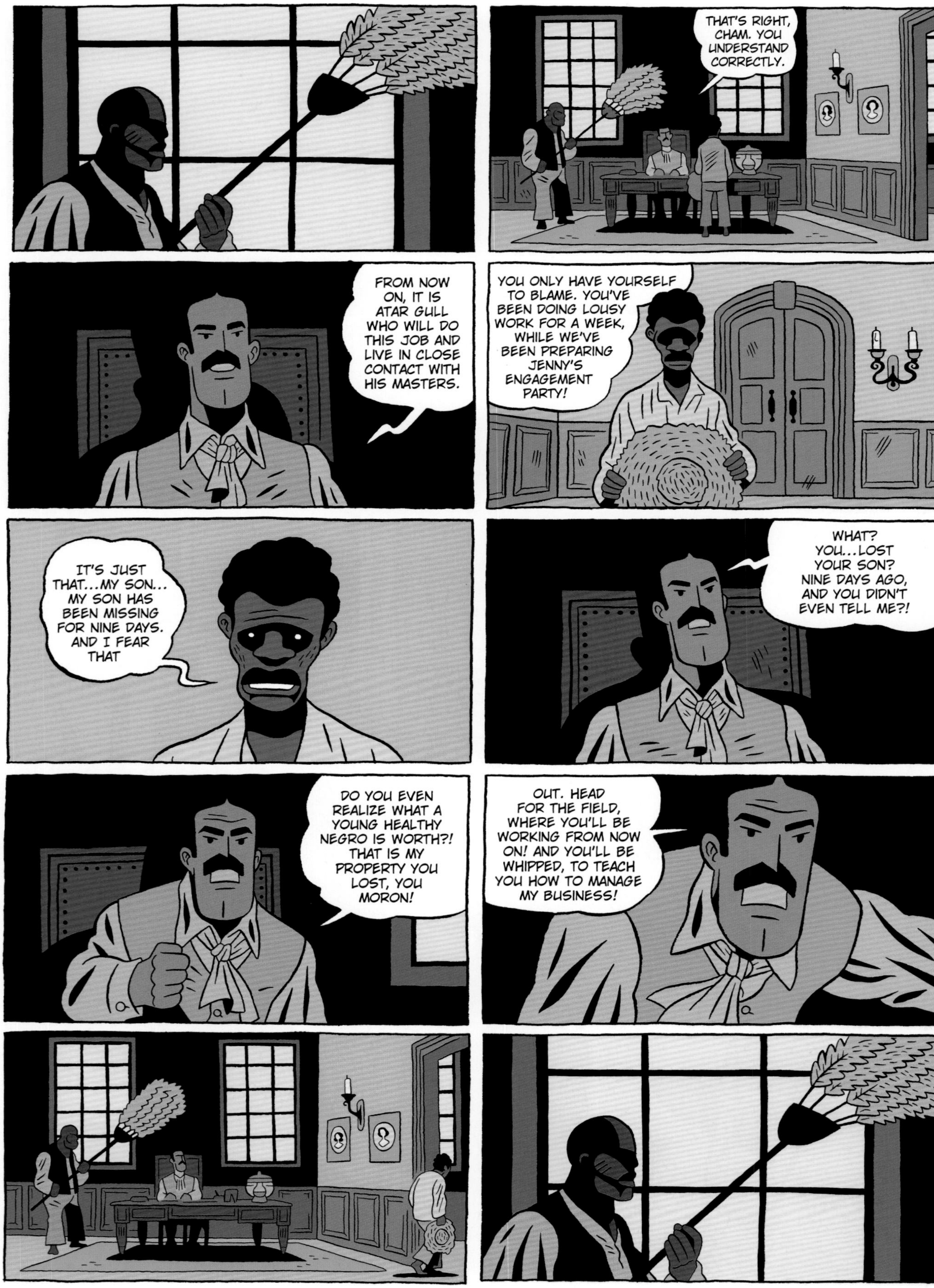
THAT'S RIGHT, CHAM. YOU UNDERSTAND CORRECTLY.
FROM NOW ON, IT IS ATAR GULL WHO WILL DO THIS JOB AND LIVE IN CLOSE CONTACT WITH HIS MASTERS.
YOU ONLY HAVE YOURSELF TO BLAME. YOU'VE BEEN DOING LOUSY WORK FOR A WEEK, WHILE WE'VE BEEN PREPARING JENNY'S ENGAGEMENT PARTY!
IT'S JUST THAT...MY SON... MY SON HAS BEEN MISSING FOR NINE DAYS. AND I FEAR THAT
WHAT? YOU...LOST YOUR SON? NINE DAYS AGO, AND YOU DIDN'T EVEN TELL ME?!
DO YOU EVEN REALIZE WHAT A YOUNG HEALTHY NEGRO IS WORTH?! THAT IS MY PROPERTY YOU LOST, YOU MORON!
OUT. HEAD FOR THE FIELD, WHERE YOU'LL BE WORKING FROM NOW ON! AND YOU'LL BE WHIPPED, TO TEACH YOU HOW TO MANAGE MY BUSINESS!

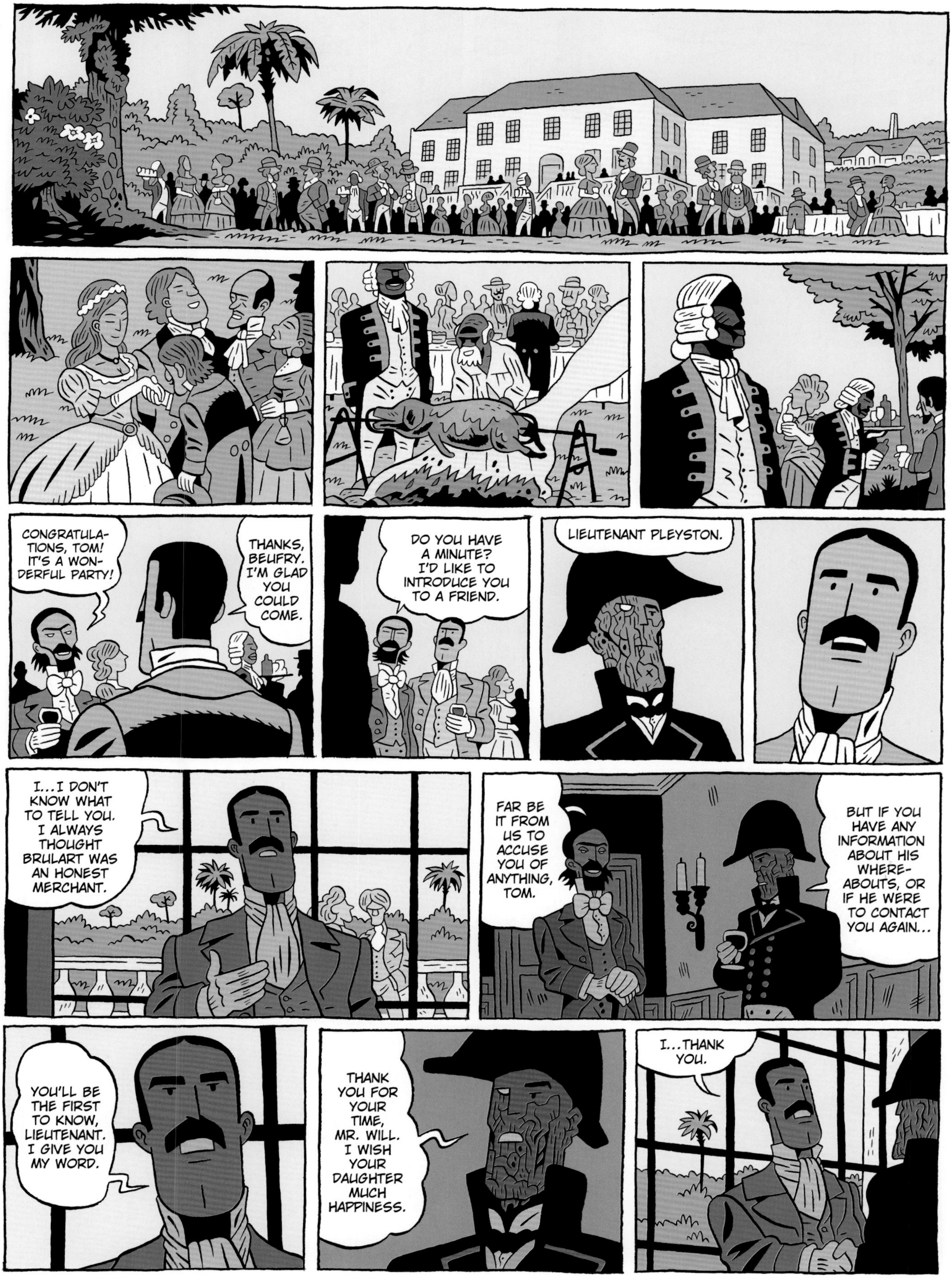
CONGRATULA-TIONS, TOM! IT'S A WON-DERFUL PARTY!
THANKS, BEUFRY. I'M GLAD YOU COULD COME.
DO YOU HAVE A MINUTE? I'D LIKE TO INTRODUCE YOU TO A FRIEND.
LIEUTENANT PLEYSTON.
I...I DON'T KNOW WHAT TO TELL YOU. I ALWAYS THOUGHT BRULART WAS AN HONEST MERCHANT.
FAR BE IT FROM US TO ACCUSE YOU OF ANYTHING, TOM.
BUT IF YOU HAVE ANY INFORMATION ABOUT HIS WHERE-ABOUTS, OR IF HE WERE TO CONTACT YOU AGAIN...
YOU'LL BE THE FIRST TO KNOW, LIEUTENANT. I GIVE YOU MY WORD.
THANK YOU FOR YOUR TIME, MR. WILL. I WISH YOUR DAUGHTER MUCH HAPPINESS.
I...THANK YOU.

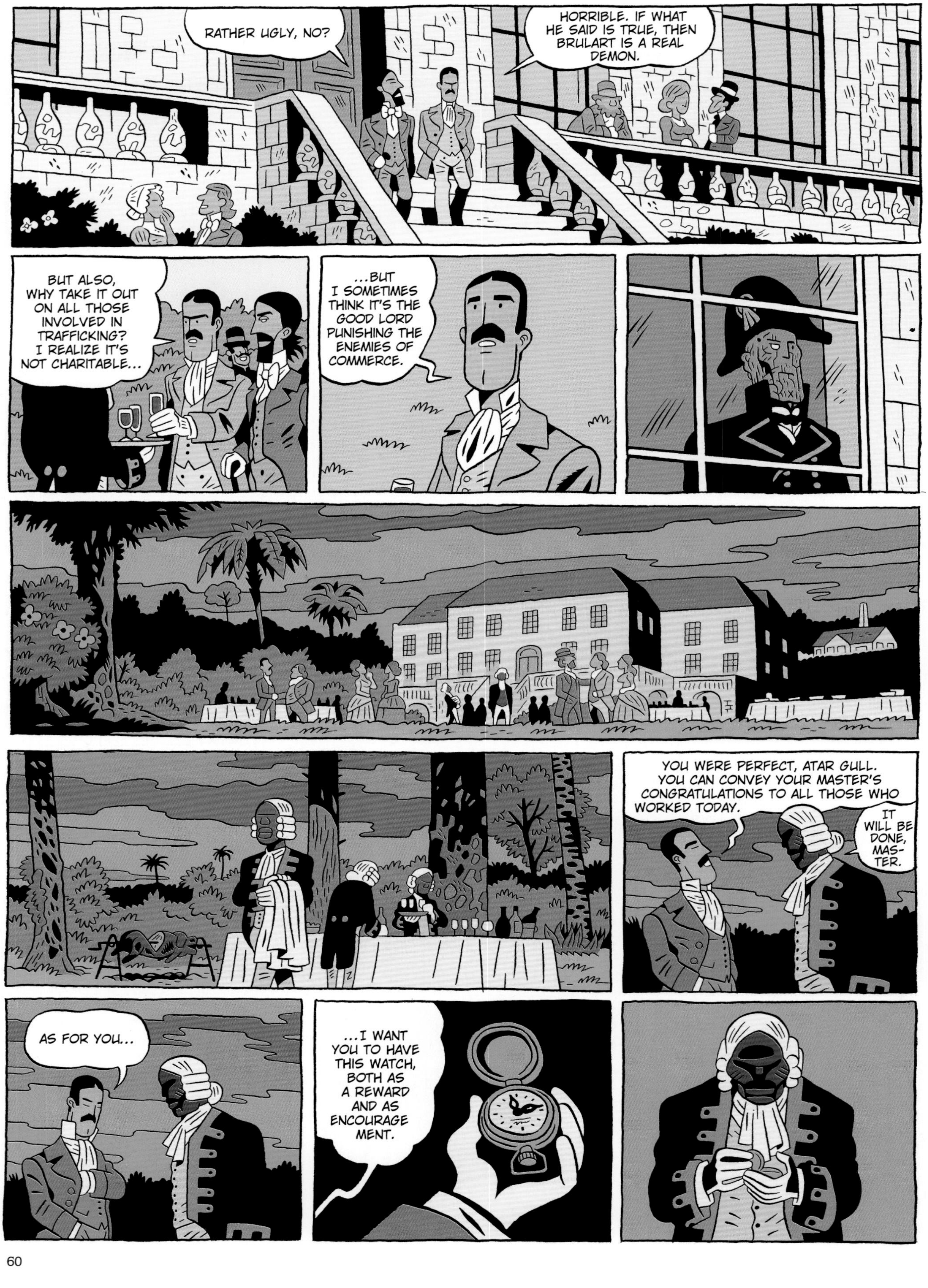
RATHER UGLY, NO?
HORRIBLE. IF WHAT HE SAID IS TRUE, THEN BRULART IS A REAL DEMON.
BUT ALSO, WHY TAKE IT OUT ON ALL THOSE INVOLVED IN TRAFFICKING? I REALIZE IT'S NOT CHARITABLE...
...BUT I SOMETIMES THINK IT'S THE GOOD LORD PUNISHING THE ENEMIES OF COMMERCE.
YOU WERE PERFECT, ATAR GULL. YOU CAN CONVEY YOUR MASTER'S CONGRATULATIONS TO ALL THOSE WHO WORKED TODAY.
IT WILL BE DONE, MAS-TER.
AS FOR YOU...
...I WANT YOU TO HAVE THIS WATCH, BOTH AS A REWARD AND AS ENCOURAGE MENT.

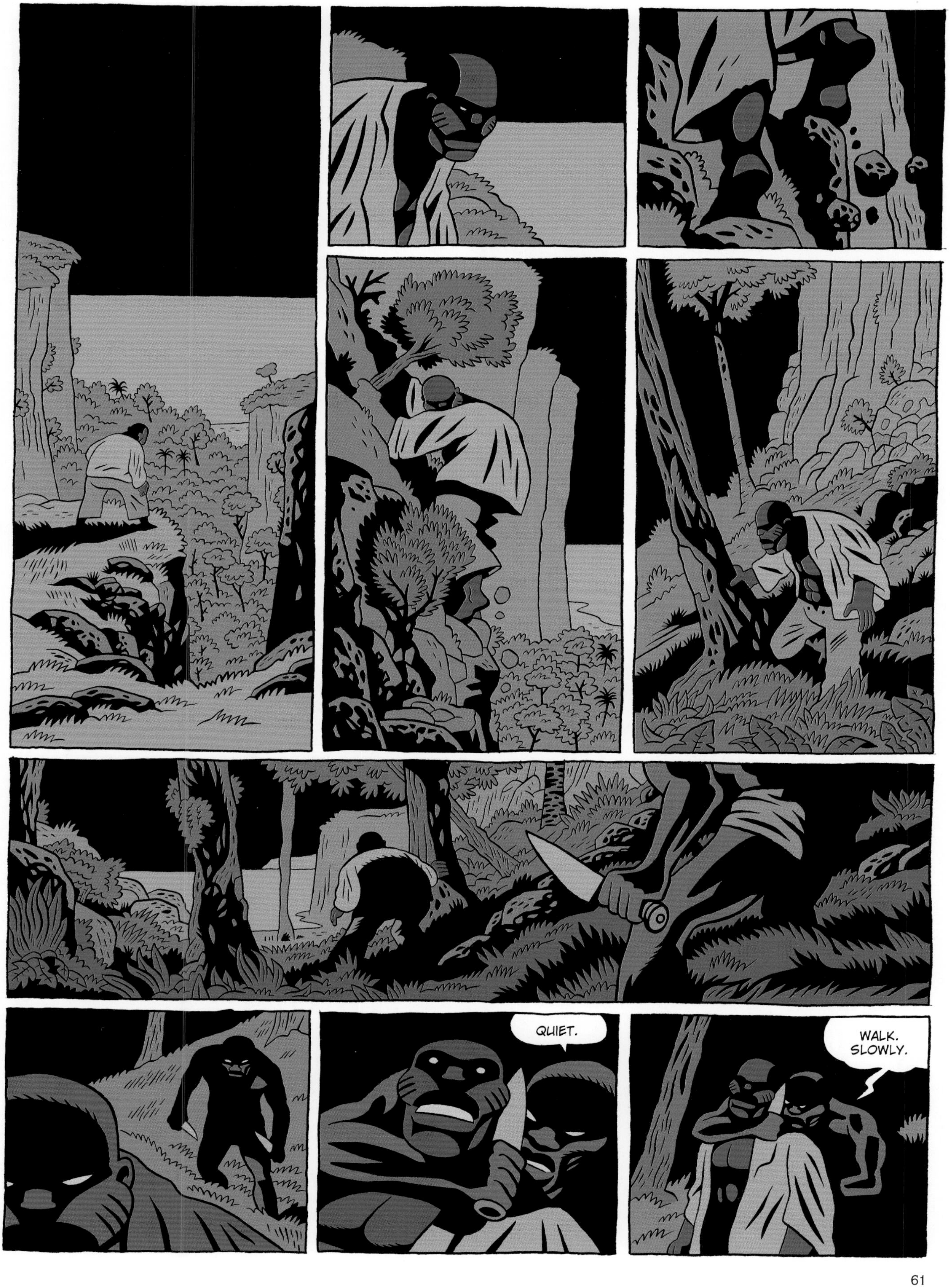
QUIET.
WALK. SLOWLY.

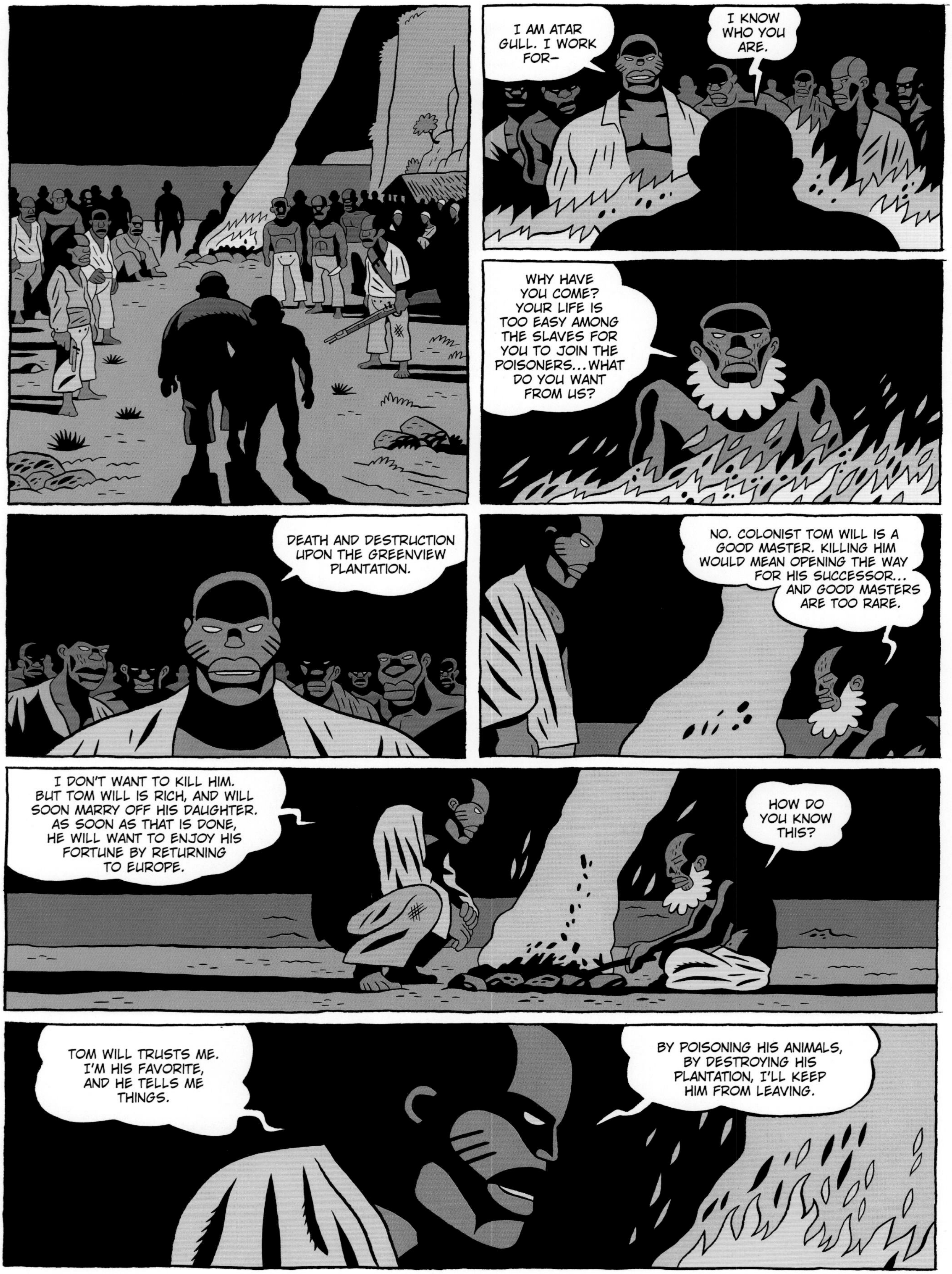
I AM ATAR GULL. I WORK FOR–
I KNOW WHO YOU ARE.
WHY HAVE YOU COME? YOUR LIFE IS TOO EASY AMONG THE SLAVES FOR YOU TO JOIN THE POISONERS...WHAT DO YOU WANT FROM US?
DEATH AND DESTRUCTION UPON THE GREENVIEW PLANTATION.
NO. COLONIST TOM WILL IS A GOOD MASTER. KILLING HIM WOULD MEAN OPENING THE WAY FOR HIS SUCCESSOR... AND GOOD MASTERS ARE TOO RARE.
I DON'T WANT TO KILL HIM. BUT TOM WILL IS RICH, AND WILL SOON MARRY OFF HIS DAUGHTER. AS SOON AS THAT IS DONE, HE WILL WANT TO ENJOY HIS FORTUNE BY RETURNING TO EUROPE.
HOW DO YOU KNOW THIS?
TOM WILL TRUSTS ME. I'M HIS FAVORITE, AND HE TELLS ME THINGS.
BY POISONING HIS ANIMALS, BY DESTROYING HIS PLANTATION, I'LL KEEP HIM FROM LEAVING.

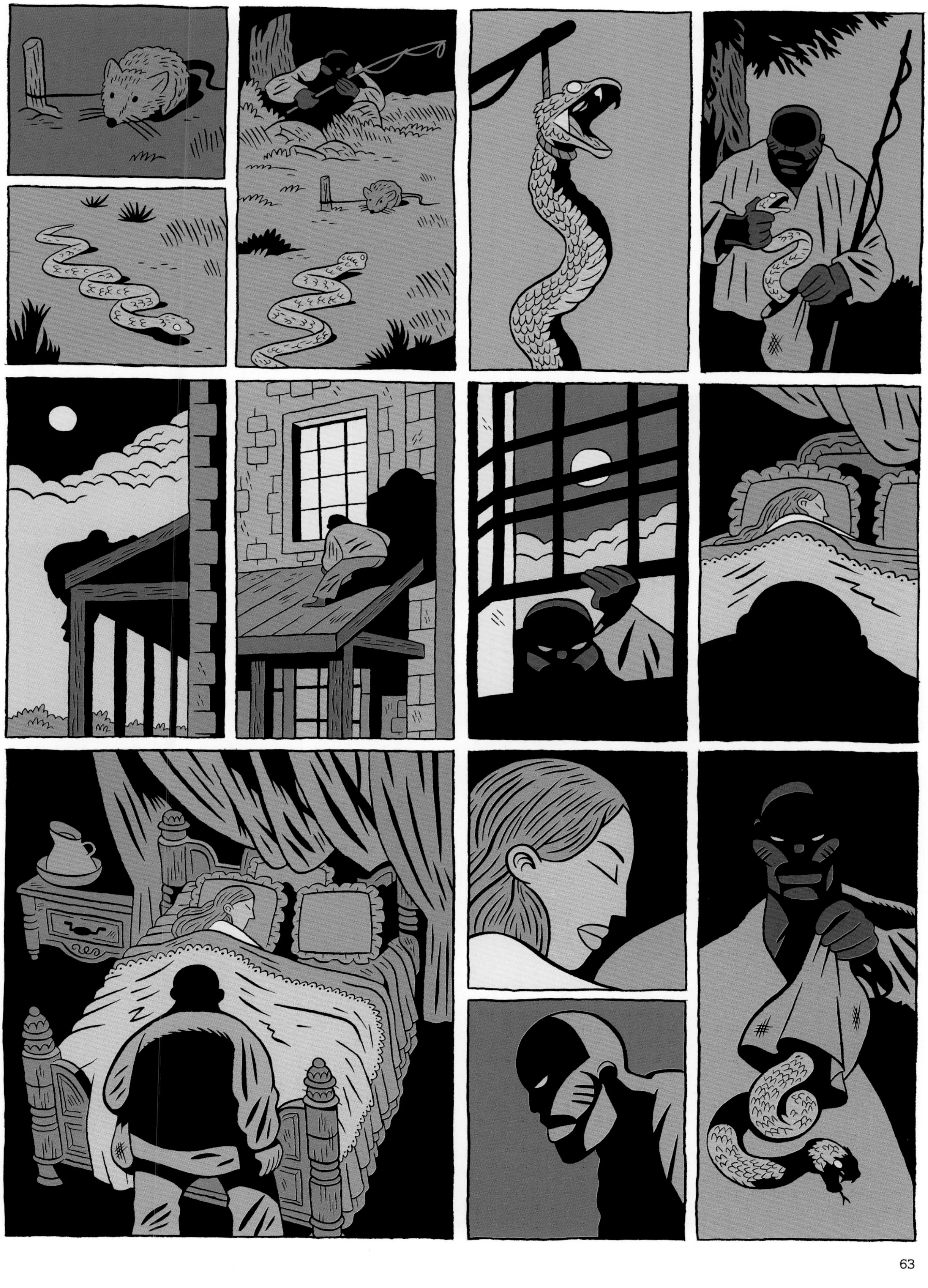

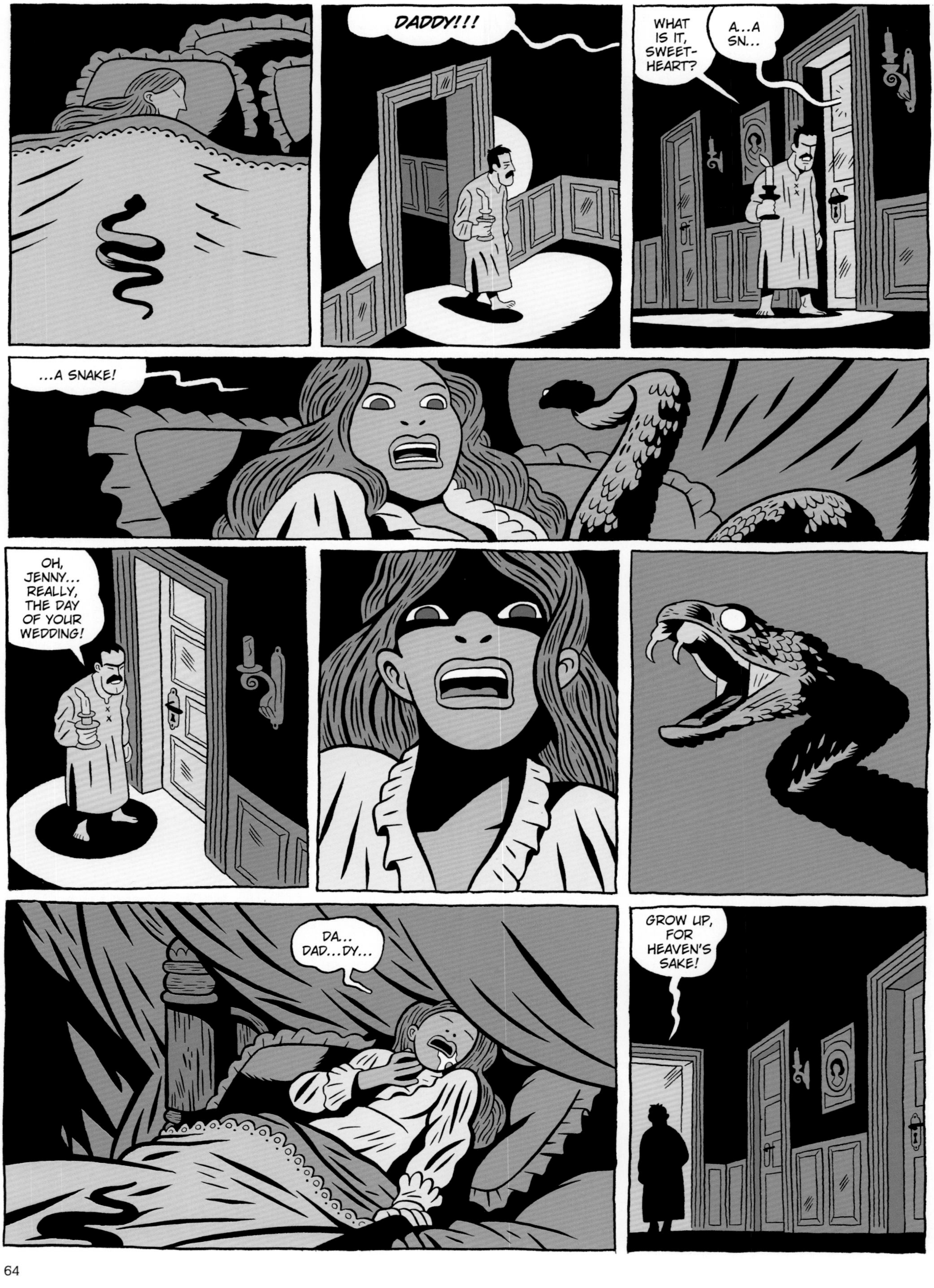
DADDY!!!
WHAT IS IT, SWEET-HEART?
A...A SN...
...A SNAKE!
OH, JENNY... REALLY, THE DAY OF YOUR WEDDING!
DA... DAD...DY...
GROW UP, FOR HEAVEN'S SAKE!

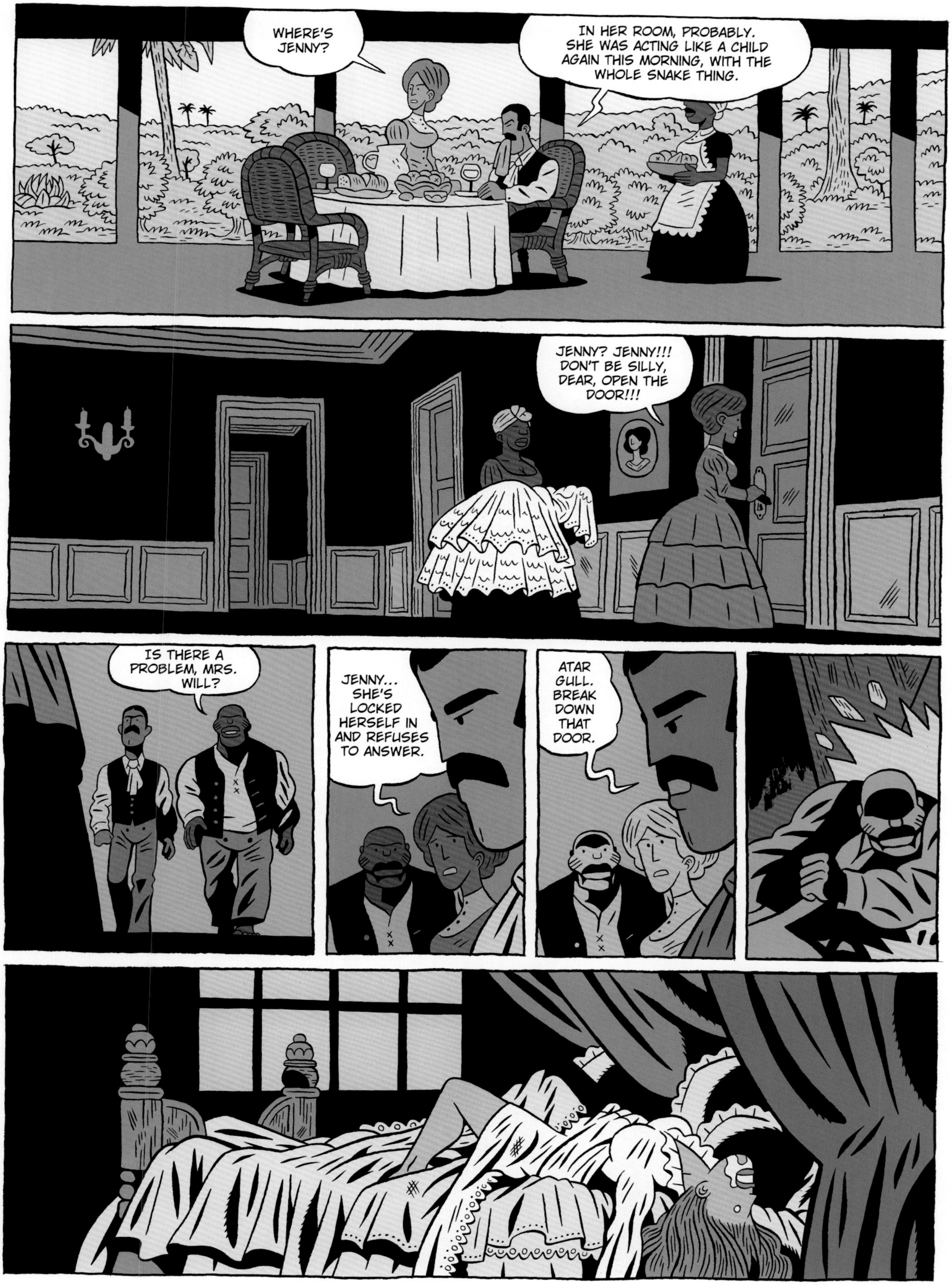
WHERE'S JENNY?
IN HER ROOM, PROBABLY. SHE WAS ACTING LIKE A CHILD AGAIN THIS MORNING, WITH THE WHOLE SNAKE THING.
JENNY? JENNY!!! DON'T BE SILLY, DEAR, OPEN THE DOOR!!!
IS THERE A PROBLEM, MRS. WILL?
JENNY... SHE'S LOCKED HERSELF IN AND REFUSES TO ANSWER.
ATAR GULL. BREAK DOWN THAT DOOR.

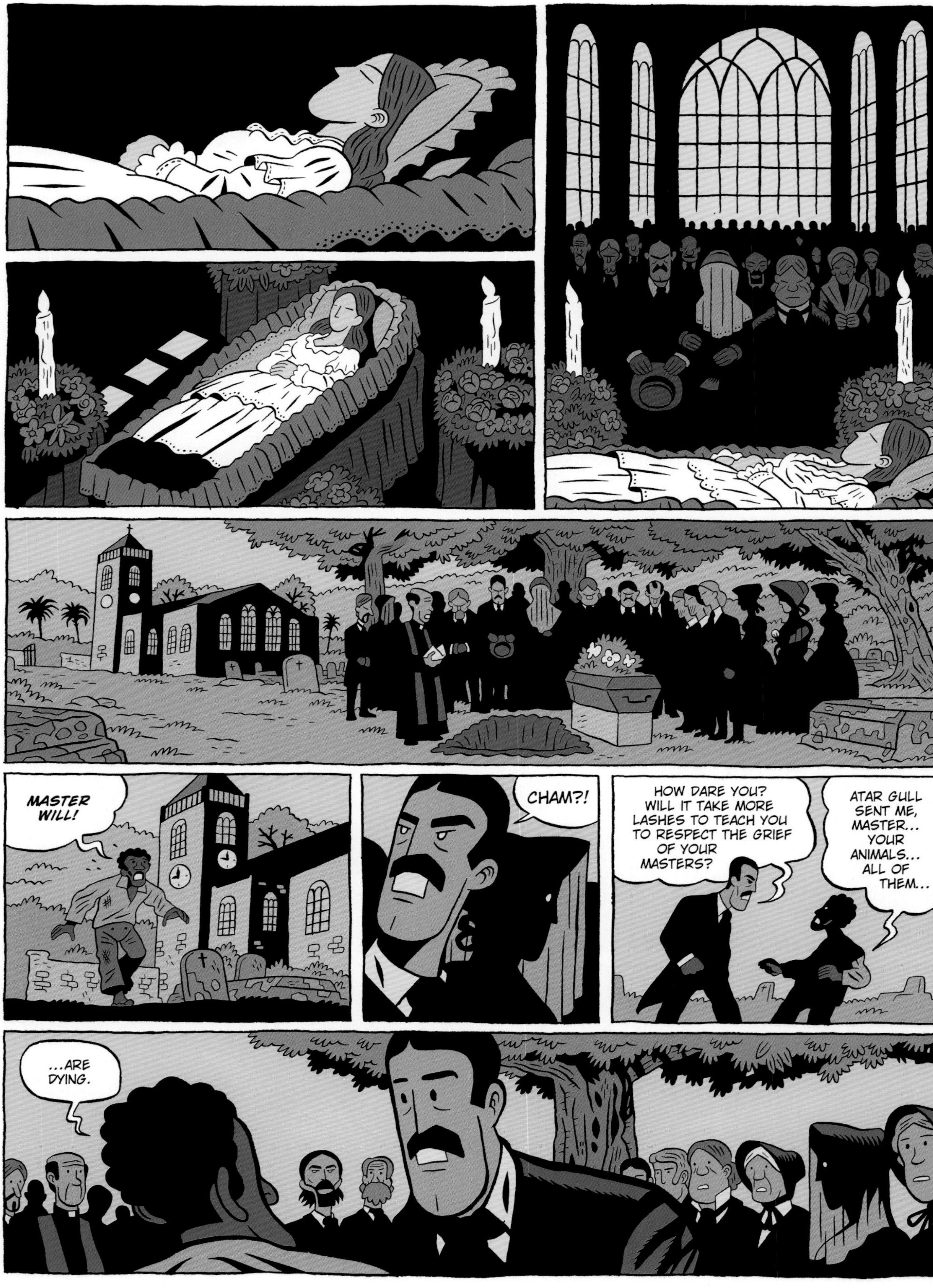
MASTER WILL!
CHAM?!
HOW DARE YOU? WILL IT TAKE MORE LASHES TO TEACH YOU TO RESPECT THE GRIEF OF YOUR MASTERS?
ATAR GULL SENT ME, MASTER... YOUR ANIMALS... ALL OF THEM...
...ARE DYING.

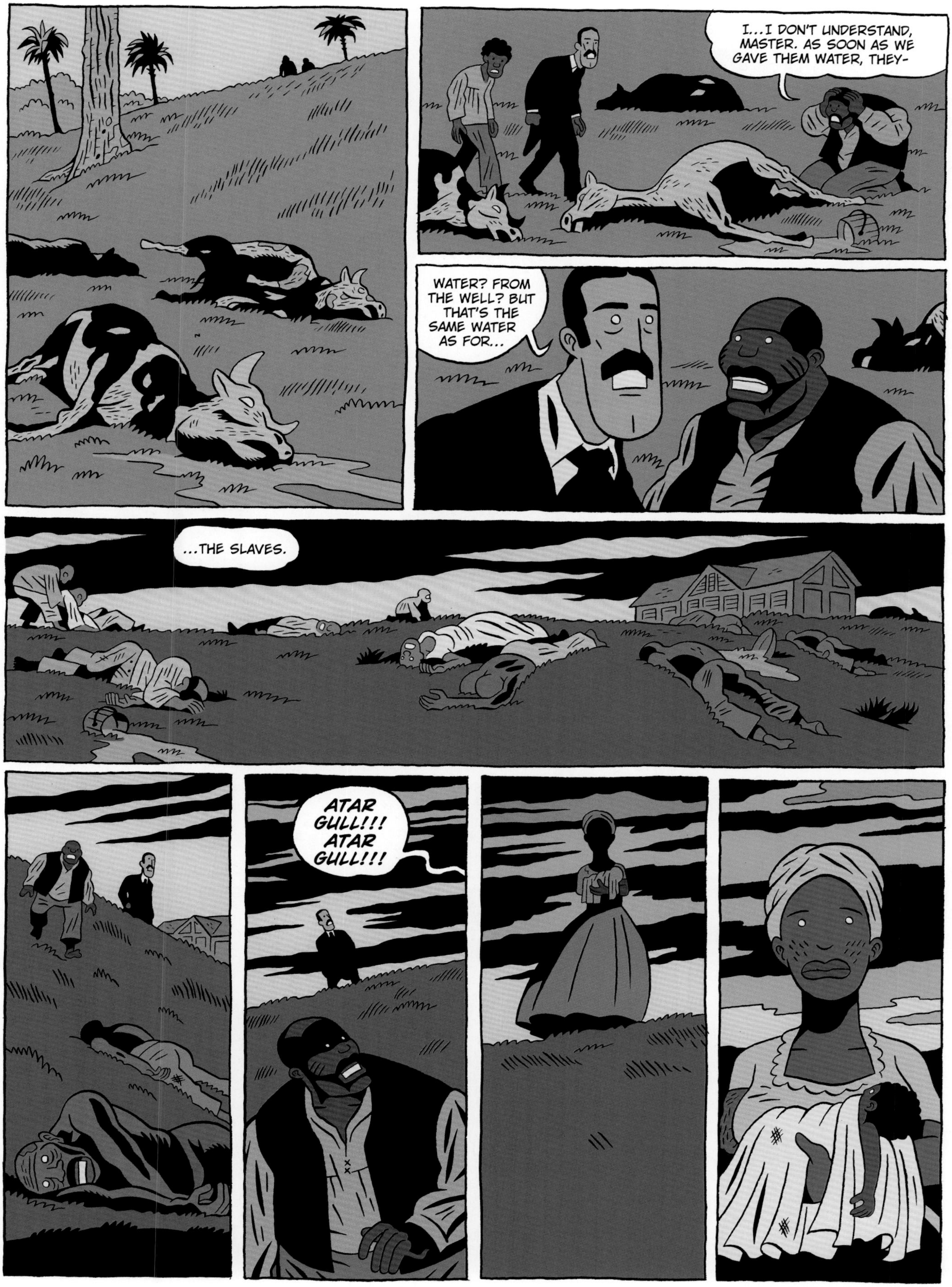

I...I DON'T UNDERSTAND, MASTER. AS SOON AS WE GAVE THEM WATER, THEY-
WATER? FROM THE WELL? BUT THAT'S THE SAME WATER AS FOR...
...THE SLAVES.
ATAR GULL!!! ATAR GULL!!!

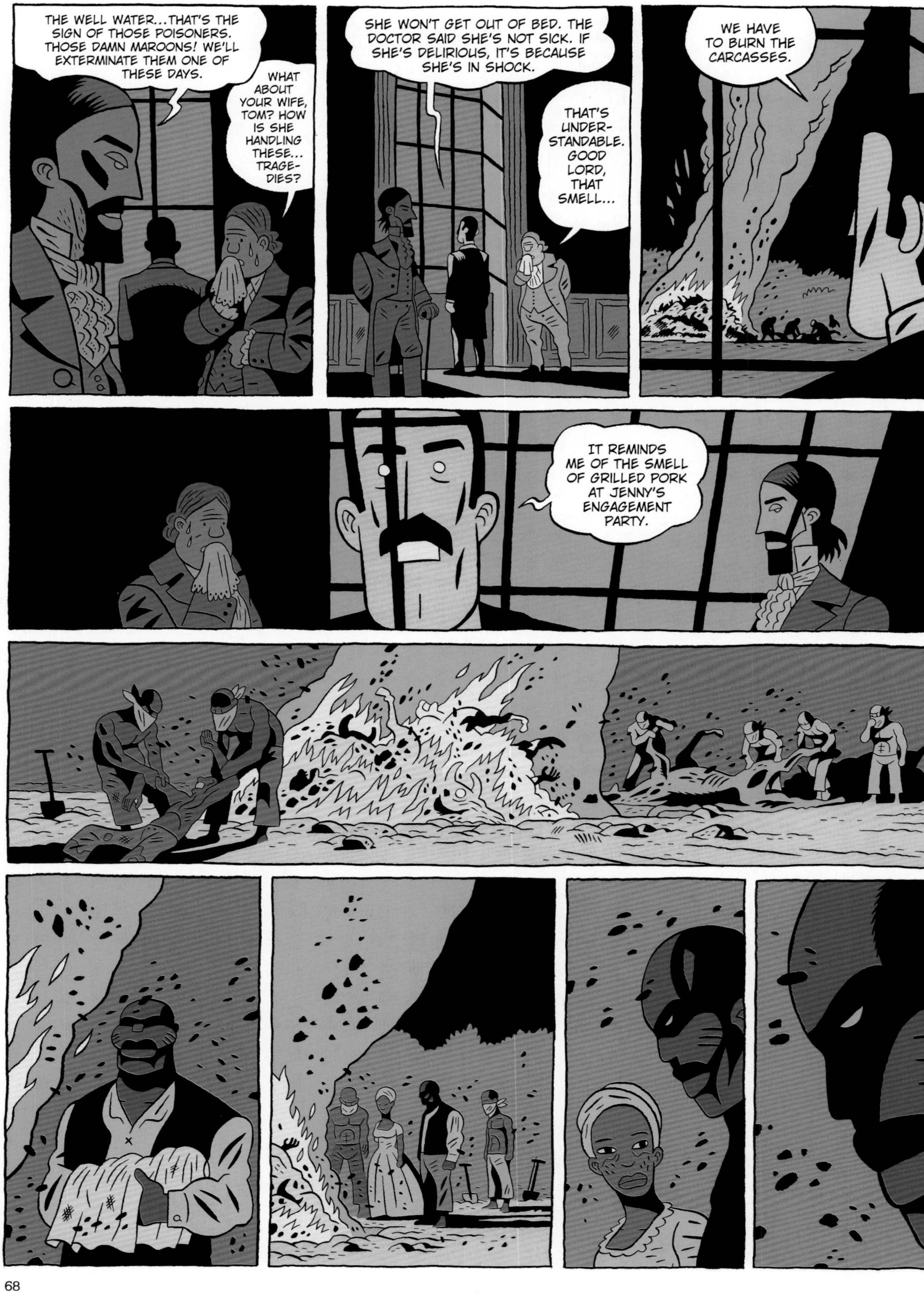
THE WELL WATER...THAT'S THE SIGN OF THOSE POISONERS. THOSE DAMN MAROONS! WE'LL EXTERMINATE THEM ONE OF THESE DAYS.
WHAT ABOUT YOUR WIFE, TOM? HOW IS SHE HANDLING THESE... TRAGEDIES?
SHE WON'T GET OUT OF BED. THE DOCTOR SAID SHE'S NOT SICK. IF SHE'S DELIRIOUS, IT'S BECAUSE SHE'S IN SHOCK.
THAT'S UNDERSTANDABLE. GOOD LORD, THAT SMELL...
WE HAVE TO BURN THE CARCASSES.
IT REMINDS ME OF THE SMELL OF GRILLED PORK AT JENNY'S ENGAGEMENT PARTY.

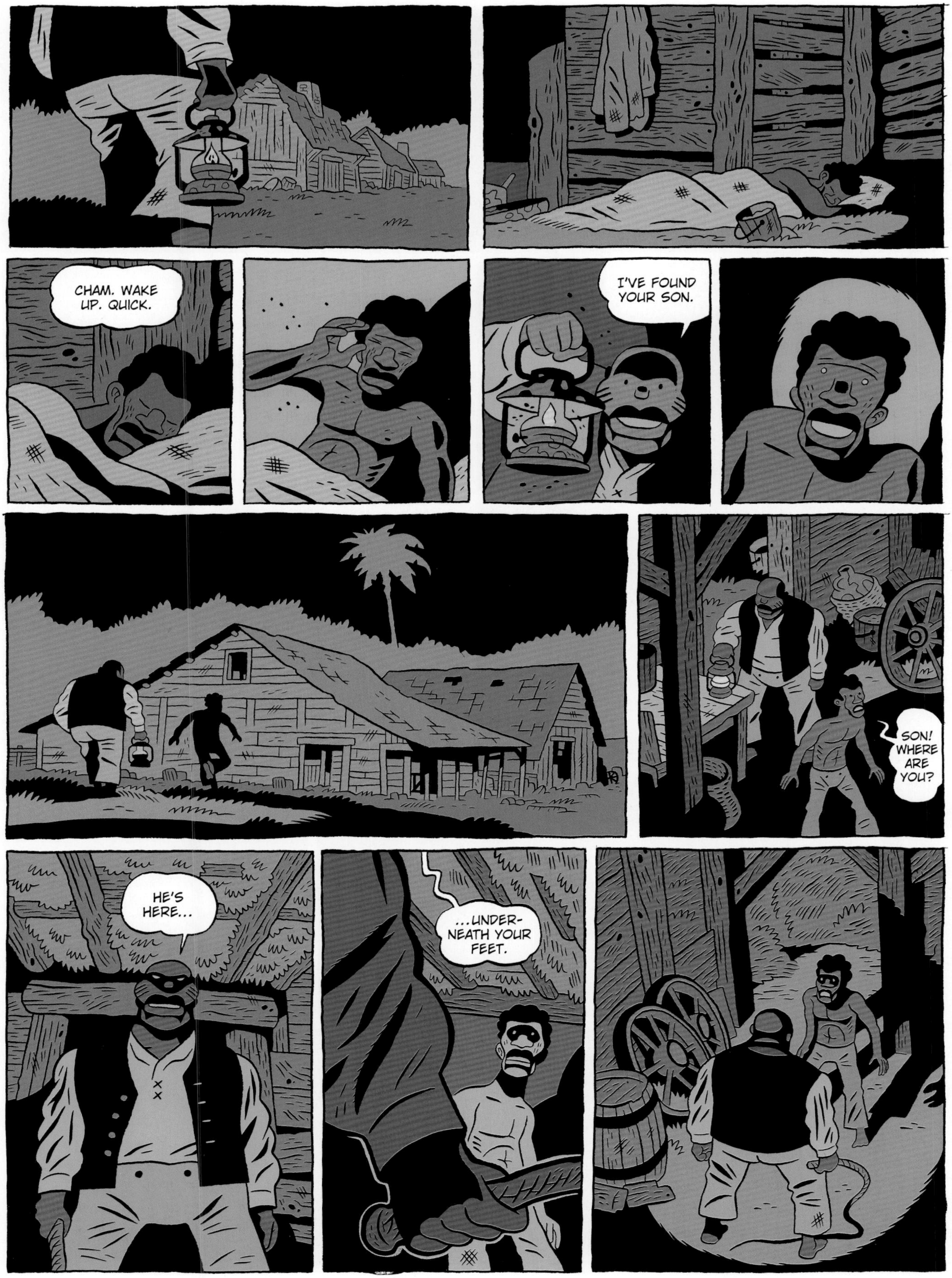
CHAM. WAKE UP. QUICK.
I'VE FOUND YOUR SON.
SON! WHERE ARE YOU?
HE'S HERE...
...UNDER-NEATH YOUR FEET.

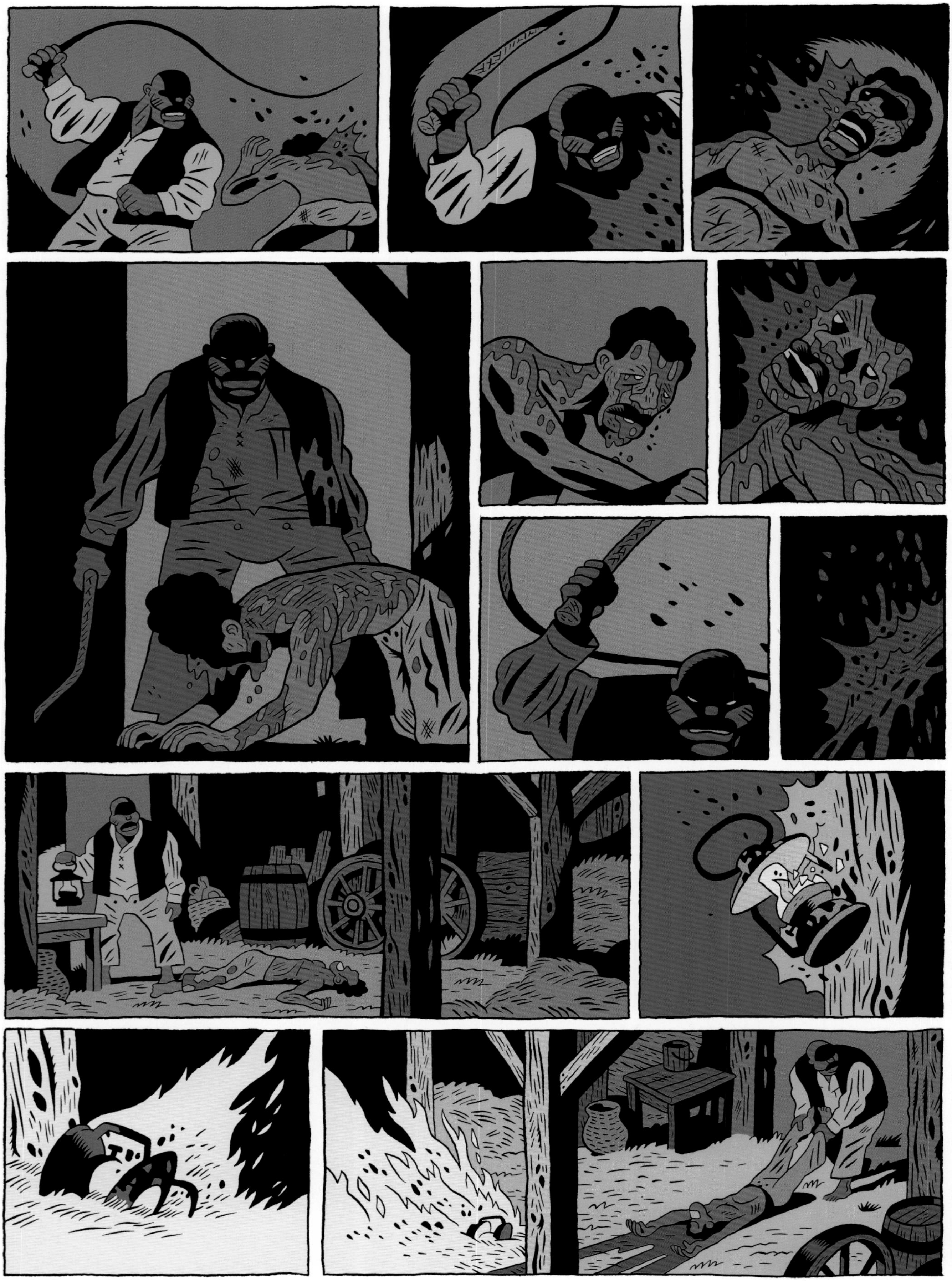

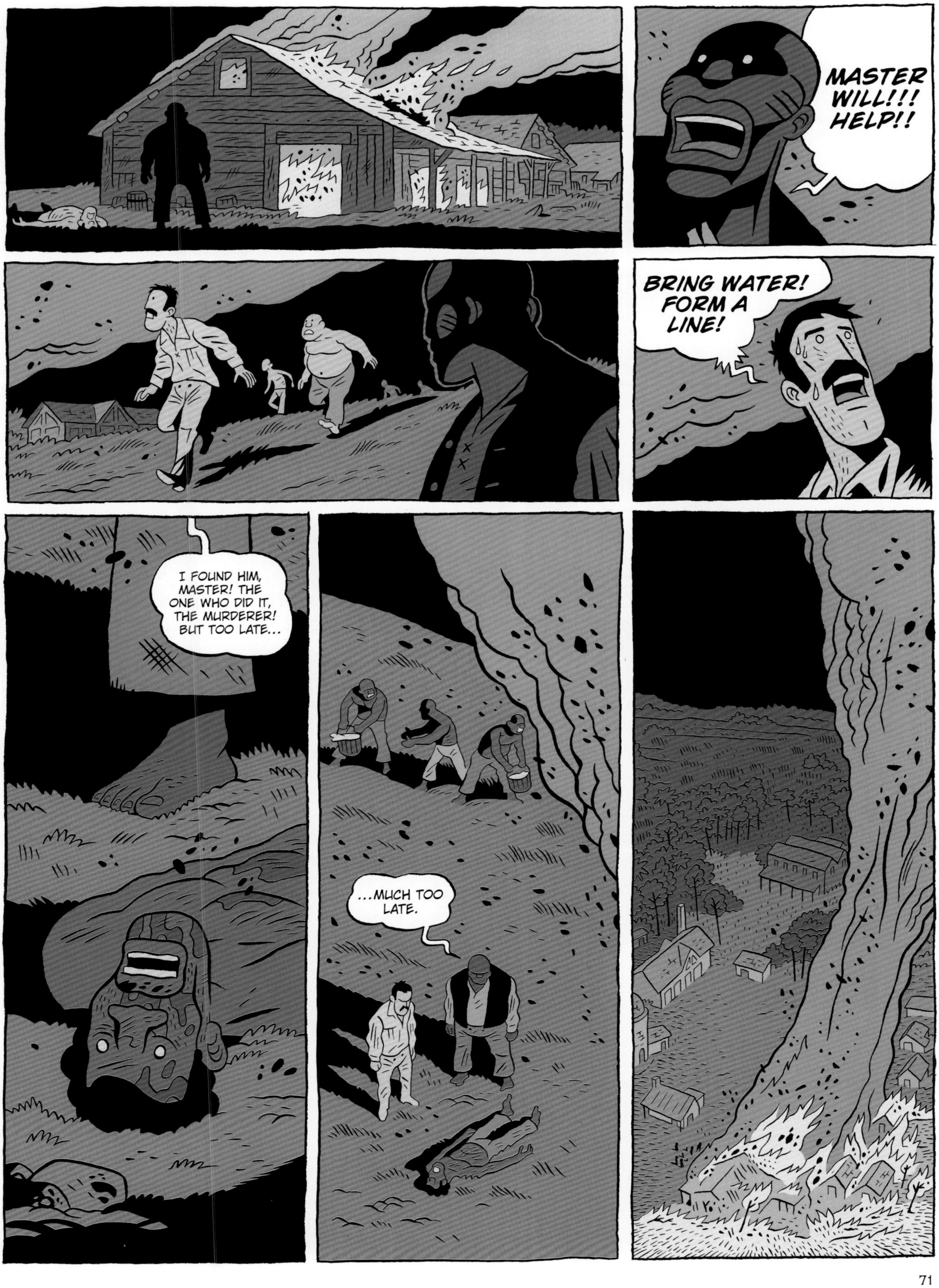
MASTER WILL!!! HELP!!
BRING WATER! FORM A LINE!
I FOUND HIM, MASTER! THE ONE WHO DID IT, THE MURDERER! BUT TOO LATE...
...MUCH TOO LATE.

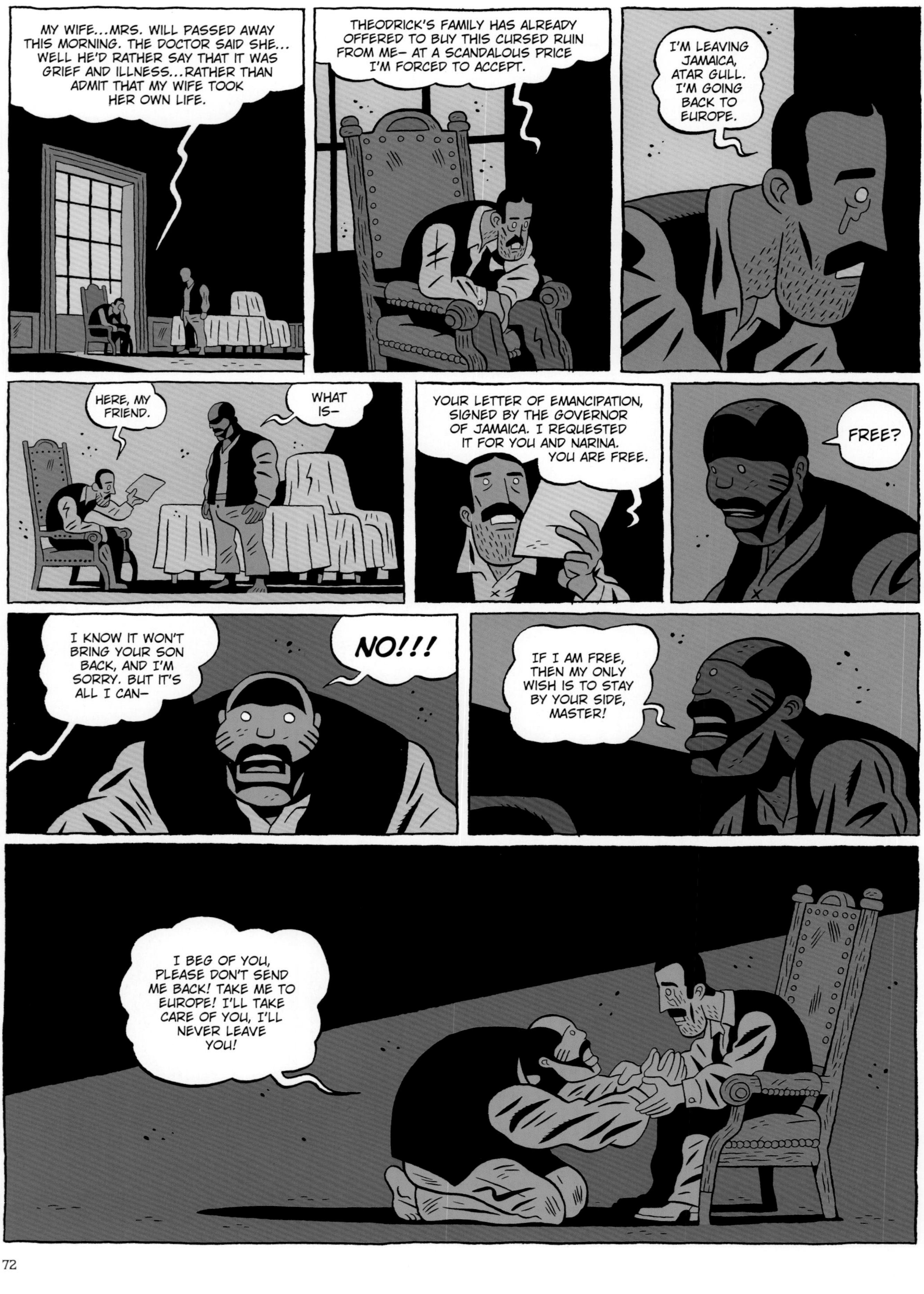

MY WIFE...MRS. WILL PASSED AWAY THIS MORNING. THE DOCTOR SAID SHE... WELL HE'D RATHER SAY THAT IT WAS GRIEF AND ILLNESS...RATHER THAN ADMIT THAT MY WIFE TOOK HER OWN LIFE.
THEODRICK'S FAMILY HAS ALREADY OFFERED TO BUY THIS CURSED RUIN FROM ME– AT A SCANDALOUS PRICE I'M FORCED TO ACCEPT.
I'M LEAVING JAMAICA, ATAR GULL. I'M GOING BACK TO EUROPE.
HERE, MY FRIEND.
WHAT IS–
YOUR LETTER OF EMANCIPATION, SIGNED BY THE GOVERNOR OF JAMAICA. I REQUESTED IT FOR YOU AND NARINA. YOU ARE FREE.
FREE?
I KNOW IT WON'T BRING YOUR SON BACK, AND I'M SORRY. BUT IT'S ALL I CAN–
NO!!!
IF I AM FREE, THEN MY ONLY WISH IS TO STAY BY YOUR SIDE, MASTER!
I BEG OF YOU, PLEASE DON'T SEND ME BACK! TAKE ME TO EUROPE! I'LL TAKE CARE OF YOU, I'LL NEVER LEAVE YOU!

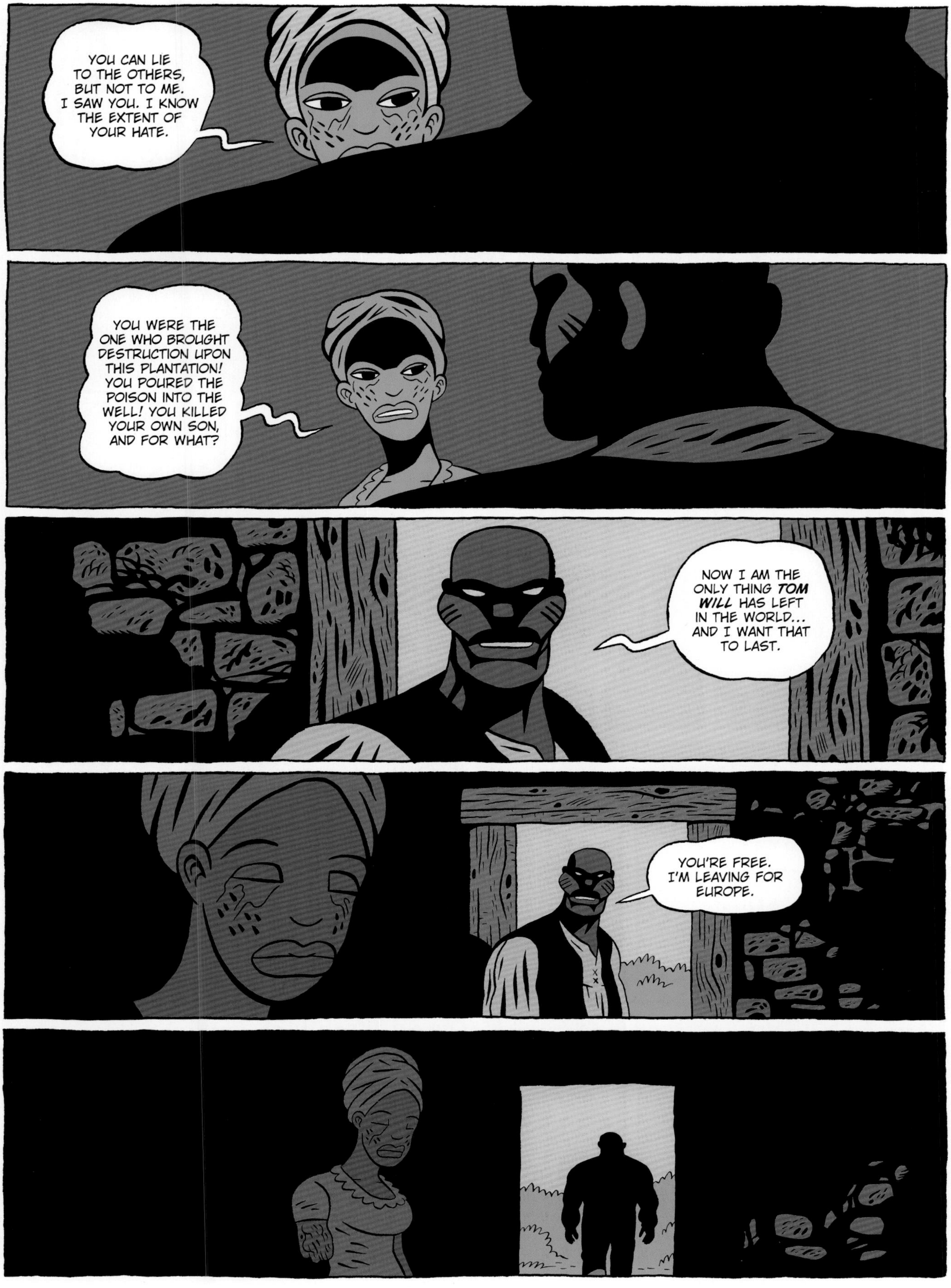
YOU CAN LIE TO THE OTHERS, BUT NOT TO ME. I SAW YOU. I KNOW THE EXTENT OF YOUR HATE.
YOU WERE THE ONE WHO BROUGHT DESTRUCTION UPON THIS PLANTATION! YOU POURED THE POISON INTO THE WELL! YOU KILLED YOUR OWN SON, AND FOR WHAT?
NOW I AM THE ONLY THING TOM WILL HAS LEFT IN THE WORLD... AND I WANT THAT TO LAST.
YOU'RE FREE. I'M LEAVING FOR EUROPE.

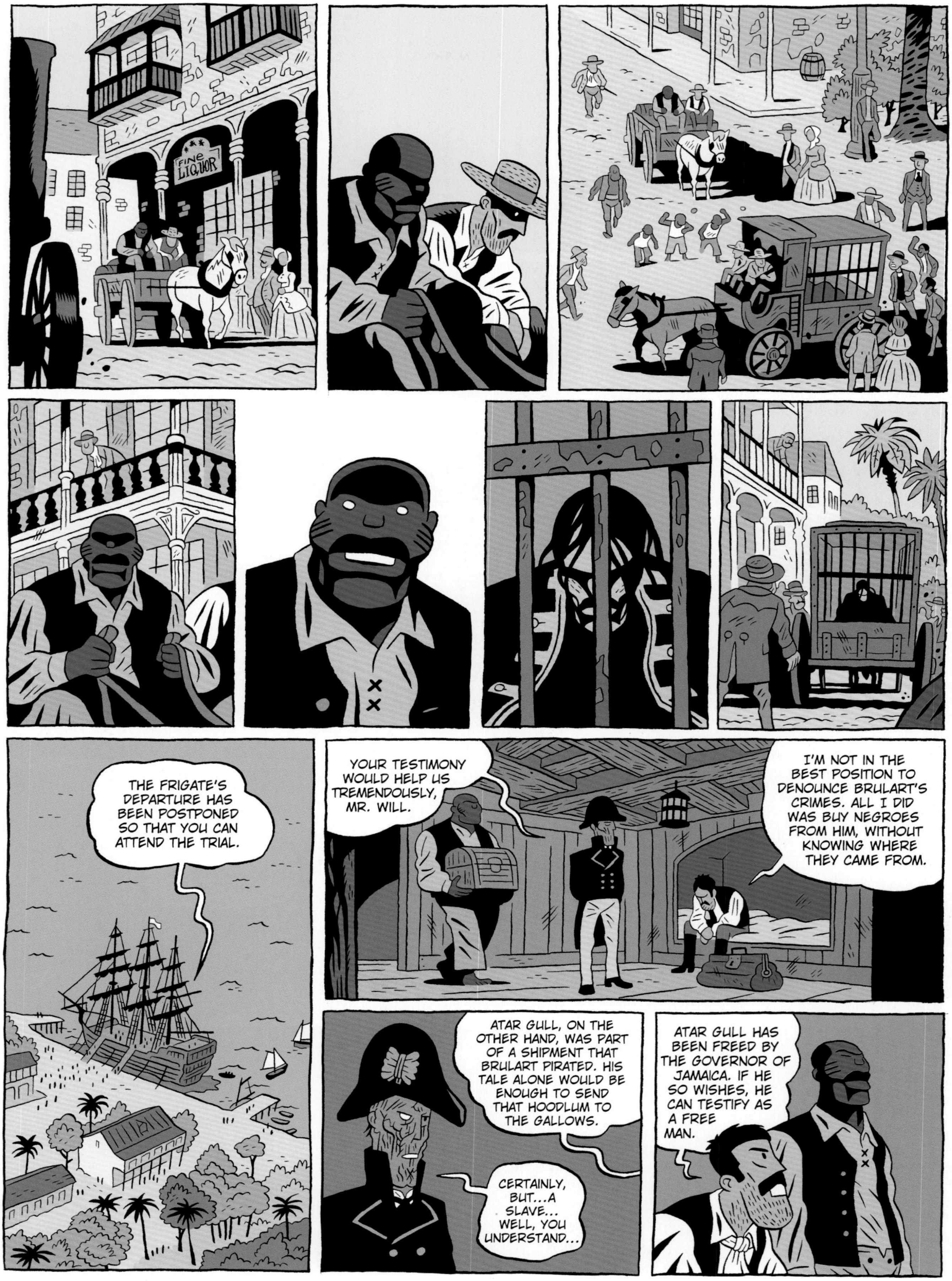
FINE LIQUOR
THE FRIGATE'S DEPARTURE HAS BEEN POSTPONED SO THAT YOU CAN ATTEND THE TRIAL.
YOUR TESTIMONY WOULD HELP US TREMENDOUSLY, MR. WILL.
I'M NOT IN THE BEST POSITION TO DENOUNCE BRULART'S CRIMES. ALL I DID WAS BUY NEGROES FROM HIM, WITHOUT KNOWING WHERE THEY CAME FROM.
ATAR GULL, ON THE OTHER HAND, WAS PART OF A SHIPMENT THAT BRULART PIRATED. HIS TALE ALONE WOULD BE ENOUGH TO SEND THAT HOODLUM TO THE GALLOWS.
CERTAINLY, BUT...A SLAVE... WELL, YOU UNDERSTAND...
ATAR GULL HAS BEEN FREED BY THE GOVERNOR OF JAMAICA. IF HE SO WISHES, HE CAN TESTIFY AS A FREE MAN.

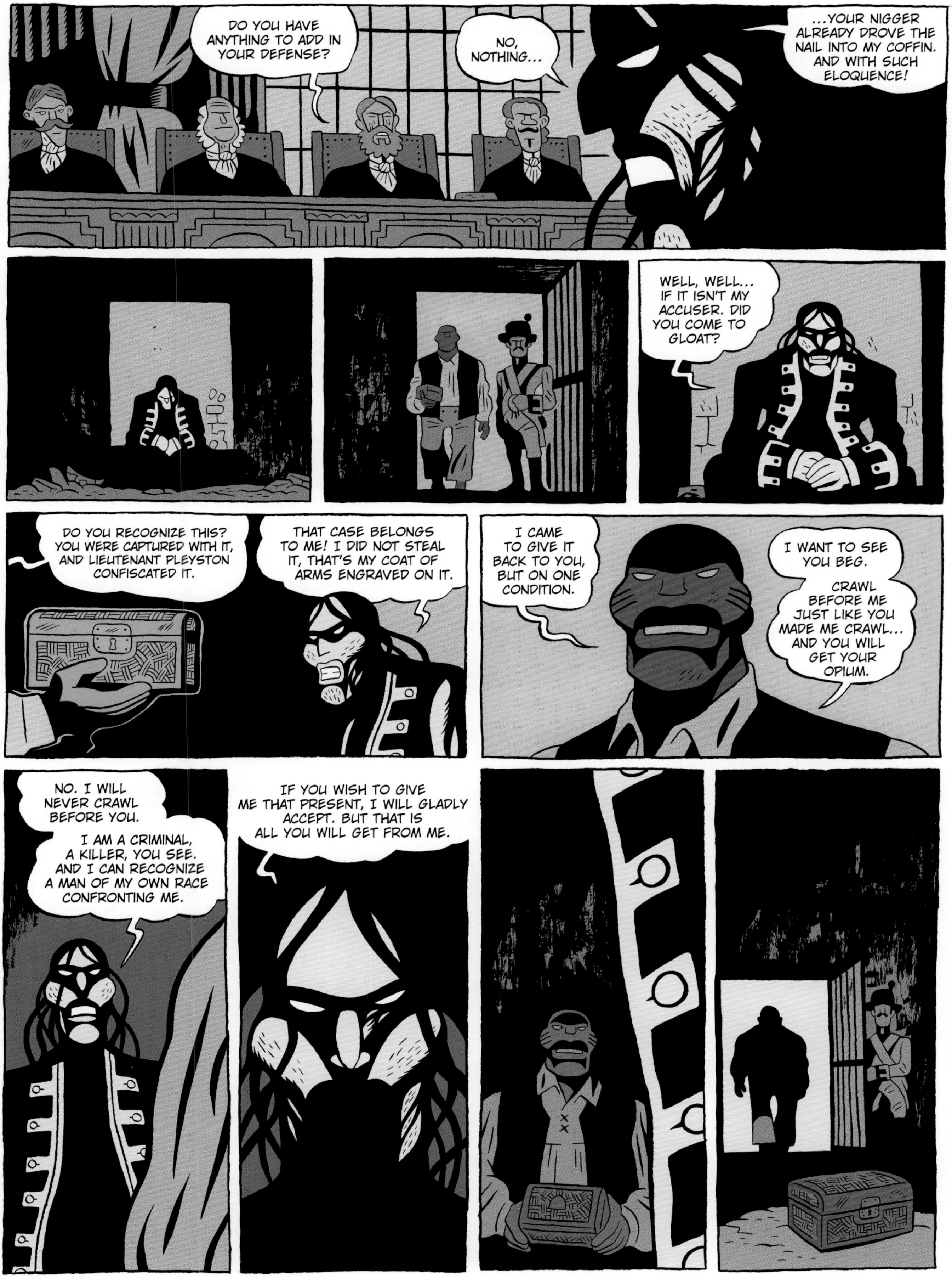
DO YOU HAVE ANYTHING TO ADD IN YOUR DEFENSE?
NO, NOTHING...
...YOUR NIGGER ALREADY DROVE THE NAIL INTO MY COFFIN. AND WITH SUCH ELOQUENCE!
WELL, WELL... IF IT ISN'T MY ACCUSER. DID YOU COME TO GLOAT?
DO YOU RECOGNIZE THIS? YOU WERE CAPTURED WITH IT, AND LIEUTENANT PLEYSTON CONFISCATED IT.
THAT CASE BELONGS TO ME! I DID NOT STEAL IT, THAT'S MY COAT OF ARMS ENGRAVED ON IT.
I CAME TO GIVE IT BACK TO YOU, BUT ON ONE CONDITION.
I WANT TO SEE YOU BEG.
CRAWL BEFORE ME JUST LIKE YOU MADE ME CRAWL... AND YOU WILL GET YOUR OPIUM.
NO. I WILL NEVER CRAWL BEFORE YOU.
I AM A CRIMINAL, A KILLER, YOU SEE. AND I CAN RECOGNIZE A MAN OF MY OWN RACE CONFRONTING ME.
IF YOU WISH TO GIVE ME THAT PRESENT, I WILL GLADLY ACCEPT. BUT THAT IS ALL YOU WILL GET FROM ME.

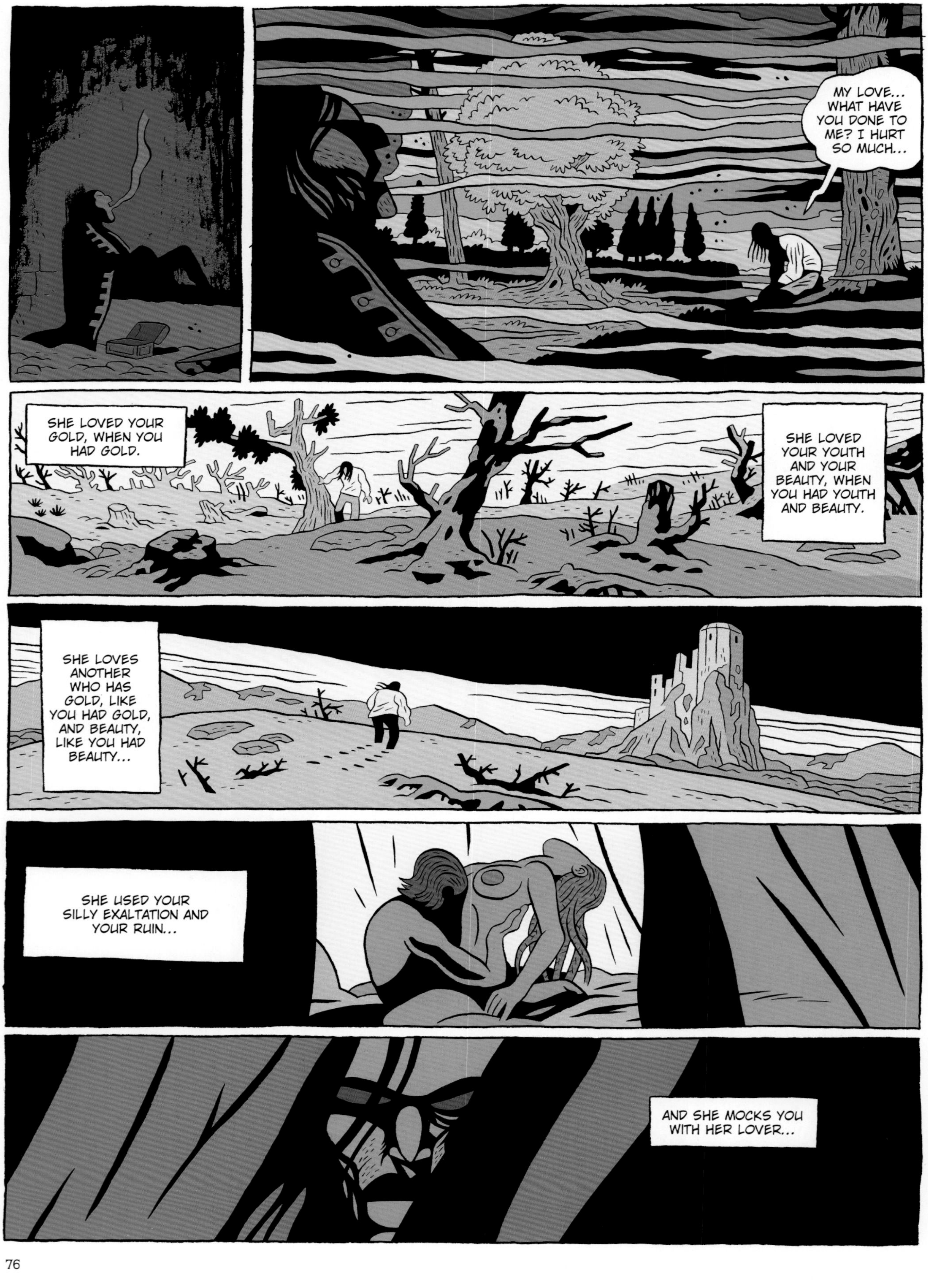
MY LOVE... WHAT HAVE YOU DONE TO ME? I HURT SO MUCH...
SHE LOVED YOUR GOLD, WHEN YOU HAD GOLD.
SHE LOVED YOUR YOUTH AND YOUR BEAUTY, WHEN YOU HAD YOUTH AND BEAUTY.
SHE LOVES ANOTHER WHO HAS GOLD, LIKE YOU HAD GOLD, AND BEAUTY, LIKE YOU HAD BEAUTY...
SHE USED YOUR SILLY EXALTATION AND YOUR RUIN...
AND SHE MOCKS YOU WITH HER LOVER...

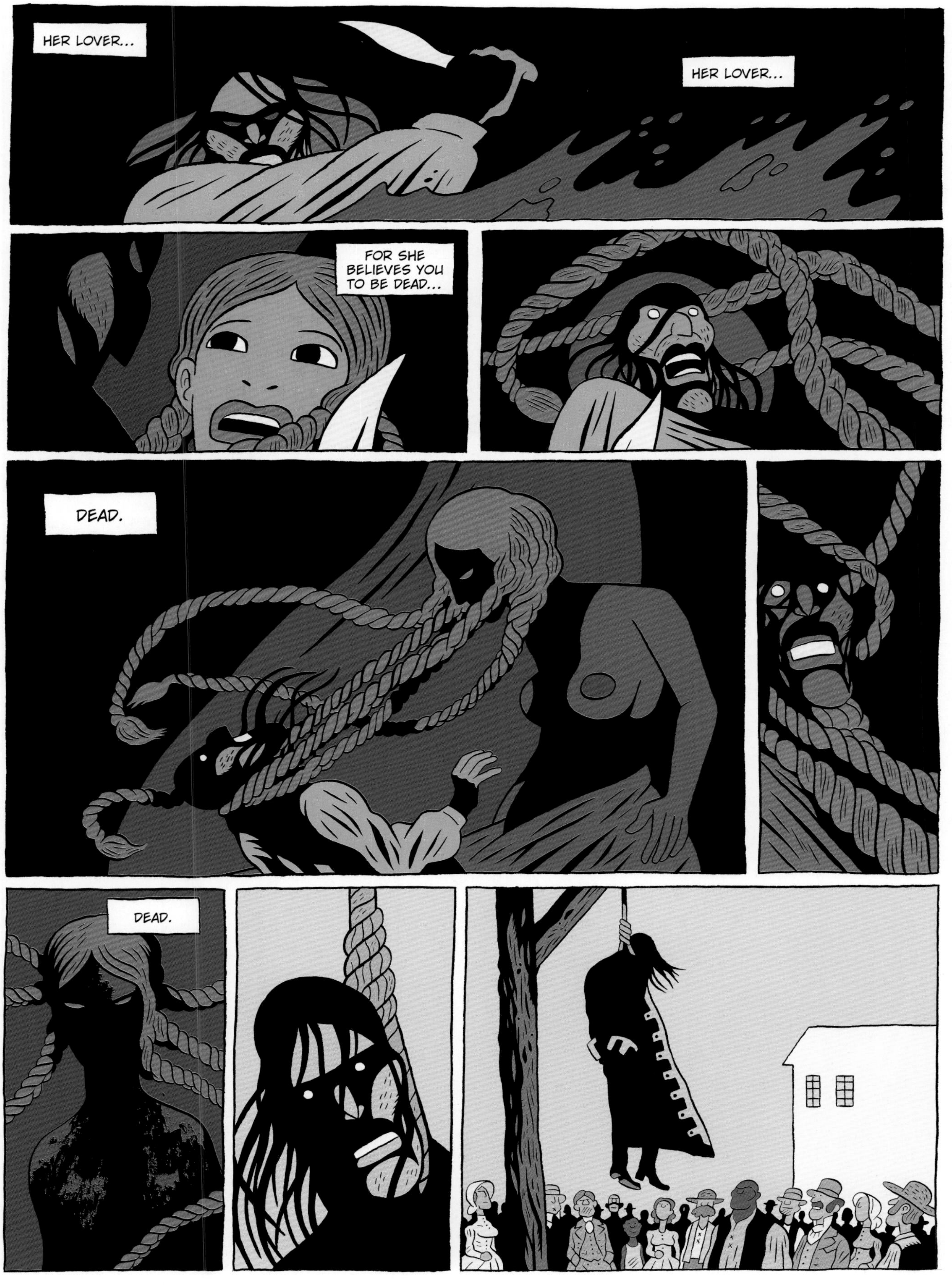
HER LOVER...
HER LOVER...
FOR SHE BELIEVES YOU TO BE DEAD...
DEAD.
DEAD.

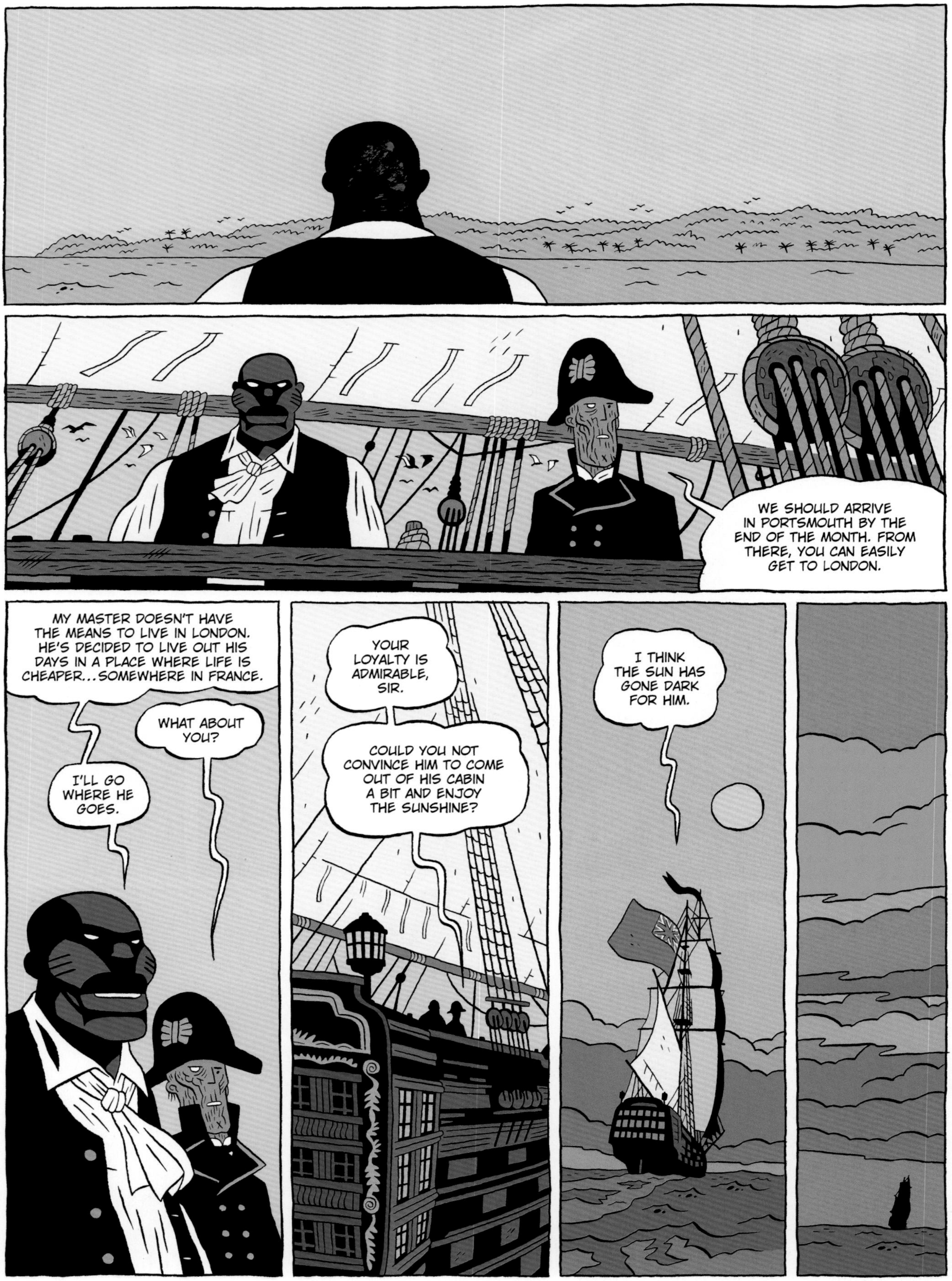
WE SHOULD ARRIVE IN PORTSMOUTH BY THE END OF THE MONTH. FROM THERE, YOU CAN EASILY GET TO LONDON.
MY MASTER DOESN'T HAVE THE MEANS TO LIVE IN LONDON. HE'S DECIDED TO LIVE OUT HIS DAYS IN A PLACE WHERE LIFE IS CHEAPER...SOMEWHERE IN FRANCE.
WHAT ABOUT YOU?
I'LL GO WHERE HE GOES.
YOUR LOYALTY IS ADMIRABLE, SIR.
COULD YOU NOT CONVINCE HIM TO COME OUT OF HIS CABIN A BIT AND ENJOY THE SUNSHINE?
I THINK THE SUN HAS GONE DARK FOR HIM.

EPILOGUE

Nantes

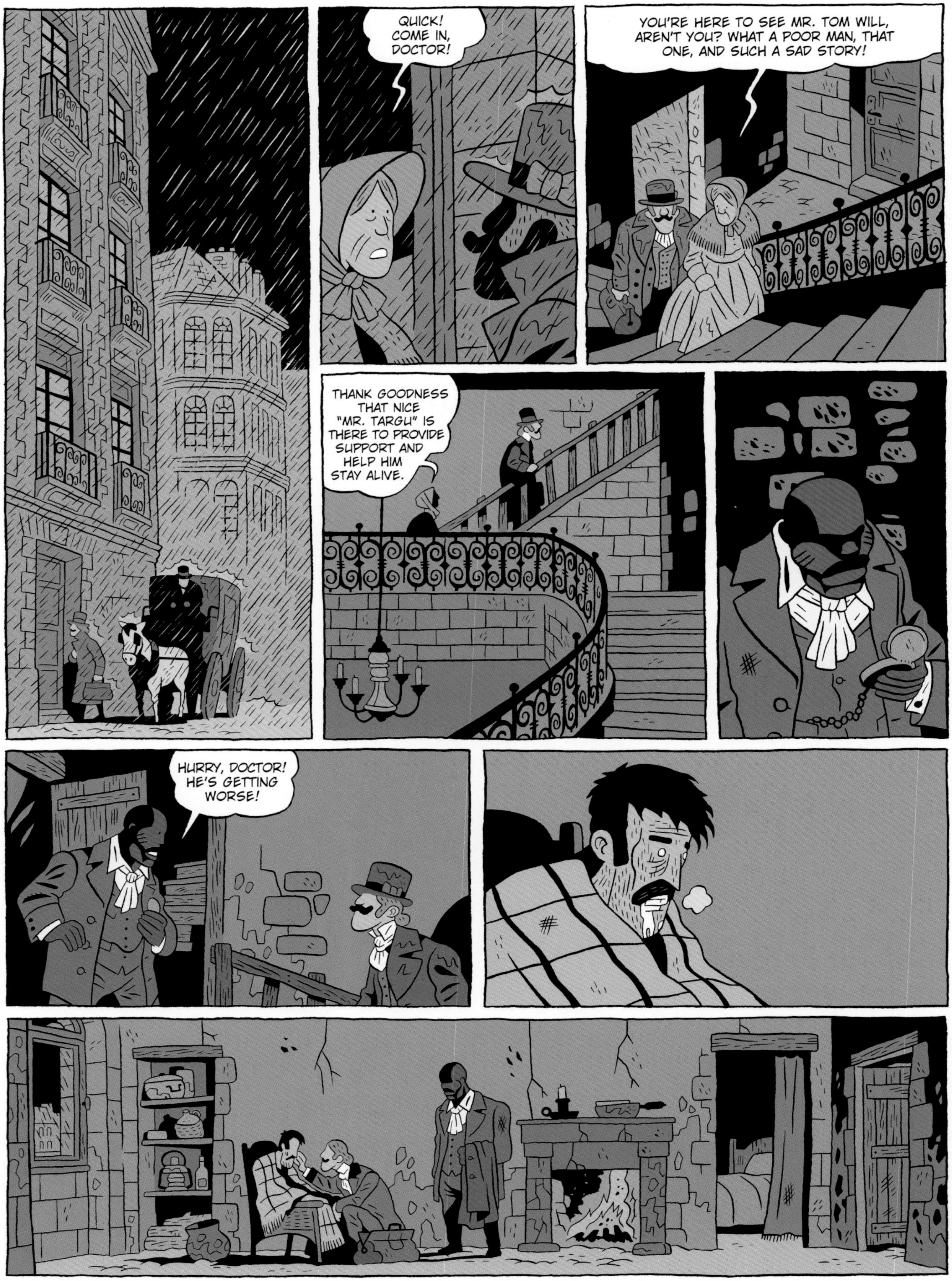
QUICK! COME IN, DOCTOR!
YOU'RE HERE TO SEE MR. TOM WILL, AREN'T YOU? WHAT A POOR MAN, THAT ONE, AND SUCH A SAD STORY!
THANK GOODNESS THAT NICE "MR. TARGU" IS THERE TO PROVIDE SUPPORT AND HELP HIM STAY ALIVE.
HURRY, DOCTOR! HE'S GETTING WORSE!

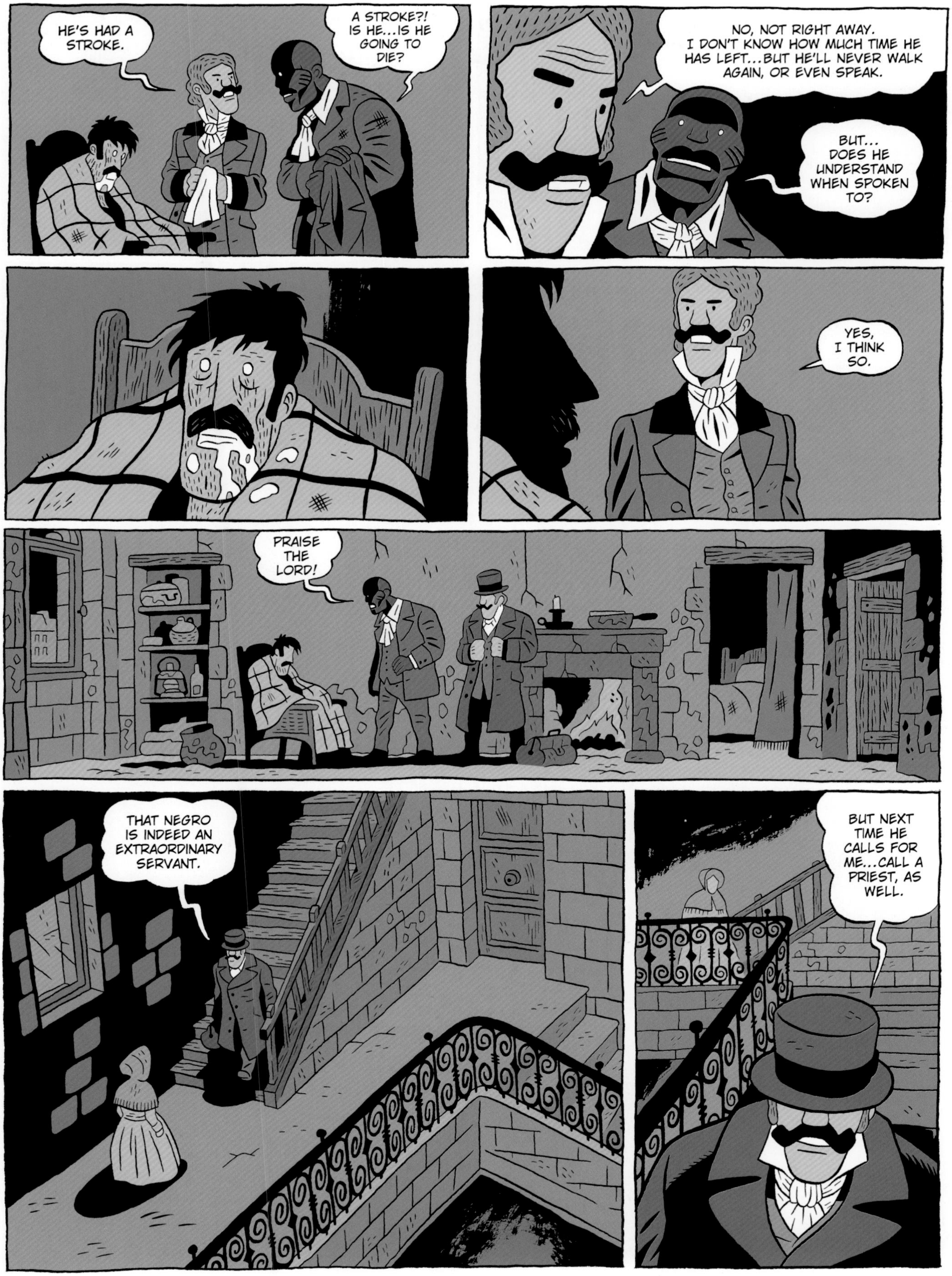
HE'S HAD A STROKE.
A STROKE?! IS HE...IS HE GOING TO DIE?
NO, NOT RIGHT AWAY. I DON'T KNOW HOW MUCH TIME HE HAS LEFT...BUT HE'LL NEVER WALK AGAIN, OR EVEN SPEAK.
BUT... DOES HE UNDERSTAND WHEN SPOKEN TO?
YES, I THINK SO.
PRAISE THE LORD!
THAT NEGRO IS INDEED AN EXTRAORDINARY SERVANT.
BUT NEXT TIME HE CALLS FOR ME...CALL A PRIEST, AS WELL.

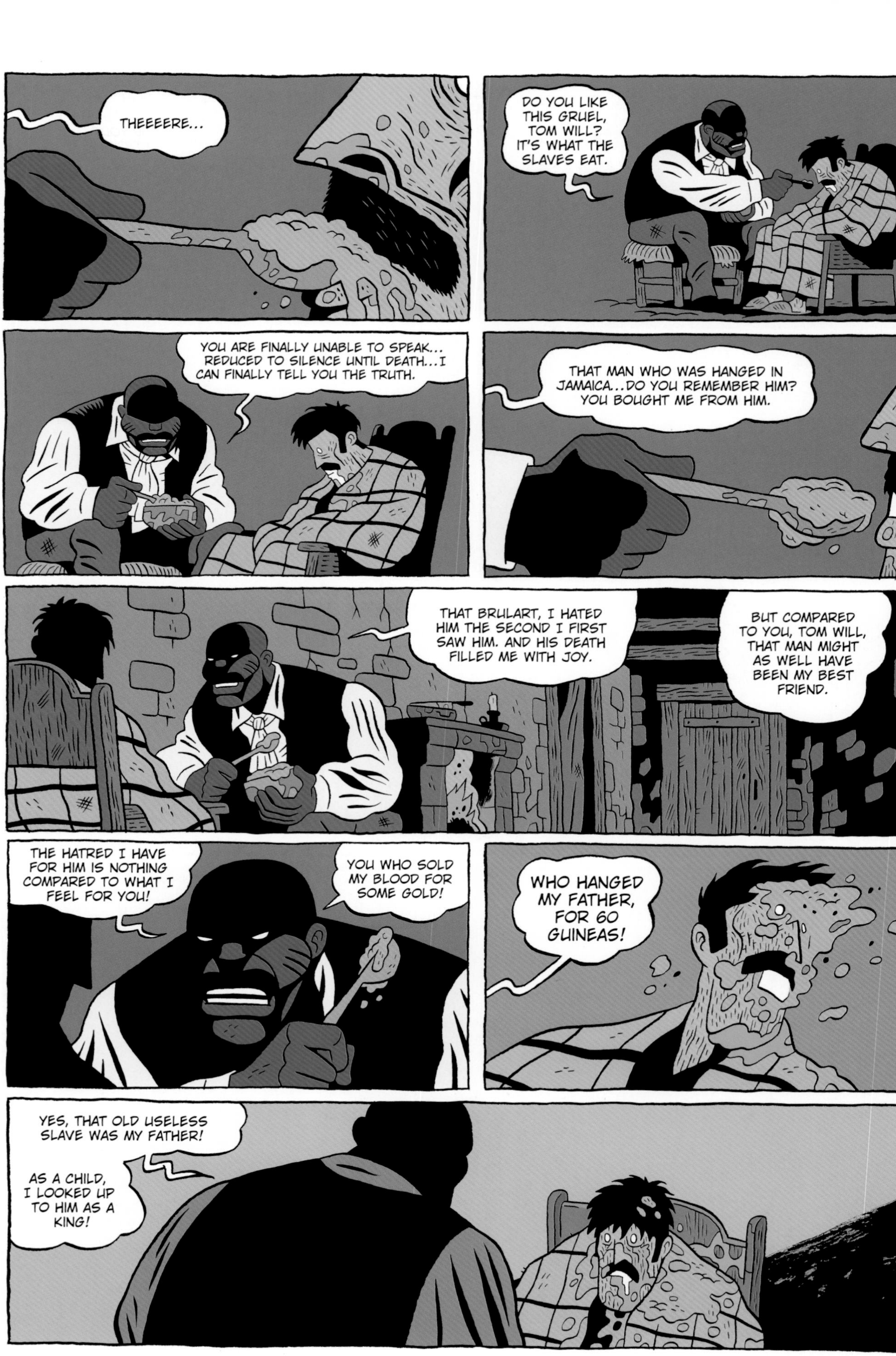
THEEEERE...
DO YOU LIKE THIS GRUEL, TOM WILL? IT'S WHAT THE SLAVES EAT.
YOU ARE FINALLY UNABLE TO SPEAK... REDUCED TO SILENCE UNTIL DEATH... I CAN FINALLY TELL YOU THE TRUTH.
THAT MAN WHO WAS HANGED IN JAMAICA...DO YOU REMEMBER HIM? YOU BOUGHT ME FROM HIM.
THAT BRULART, I HATED HIM THE SECOND I FIRST SAW HIM. AND HIS DEATH FILLED ME WITH JOY.
BUT COMPARED TO YOU, TOM WILL, THAT MAN MIGHT AS WELL HAVE BEEN MY BEST FRIEND.
THE HATRED I HAVE FOR HIM IS NOTHING COMPARED TO WHAT I FEEL FOR YOU!
YOU WHO SOLD MY BLOOD FOR SOME GOLD!
WHO HANGED MY FATHER, FOR 60 GUINEAS!
YES, THAT OLD USELESS SLAVE WAS MY FATHER!
AS A CHILD, I LOOKED UP TO HIM AS A KING!

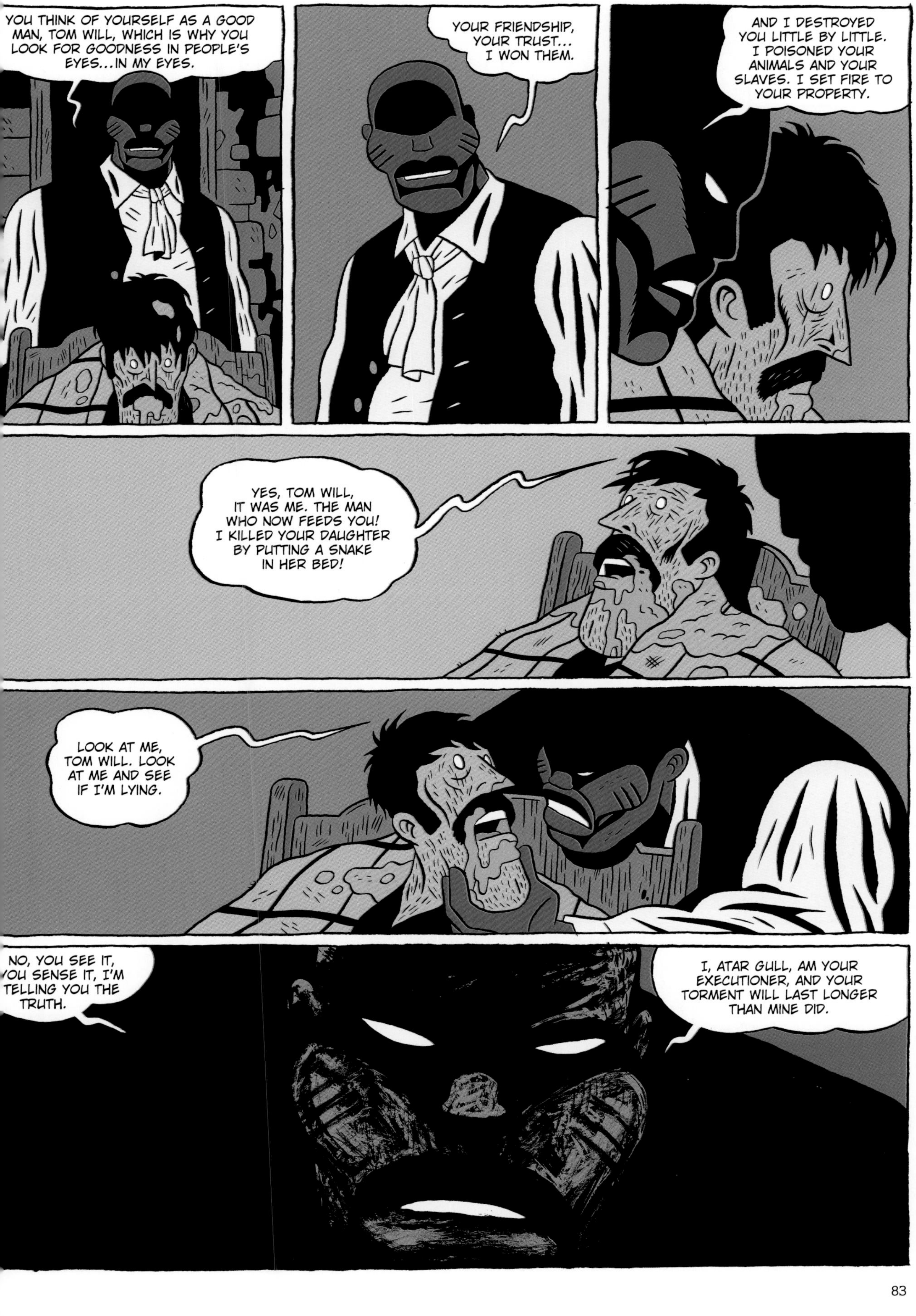
YOU THINK OF YOURSELF AS A GOOD MAN, TOM WILL, WHICH IS WHY YOU LOOK FOR GOODNESS IN PEOPLE'S EYES...IN MY EYES.
YOUR FRIENDSHIP, YOUR TRUST... I WON THEM.
AND I DESTROYED YOU LITTLE BY LITTLE. I POISONED YOUR ANIMALS AND YOUR SLAVES. I SET FIRE TO YOUR PROPERTY.
YES, TOM WILL, IT WAS ME. THE MAN WHO NOW FEEDS YOU! I KILLED YOUR DAUGHTER BY PUTTING A SNAKE IN HER BED!
LOOK AT ME, TOM WILL. LOOK AT ME AND SEE IF I'M LYING.
NO, YOU SEE IT, YOU SENSE IT, I'M TELLING YOU THE TRUTH.
I, ATAR GULL, AM YOUR EXECUTIONER, AND YOUR TORMENT WILL LAST LONGER THAN MINE DID.

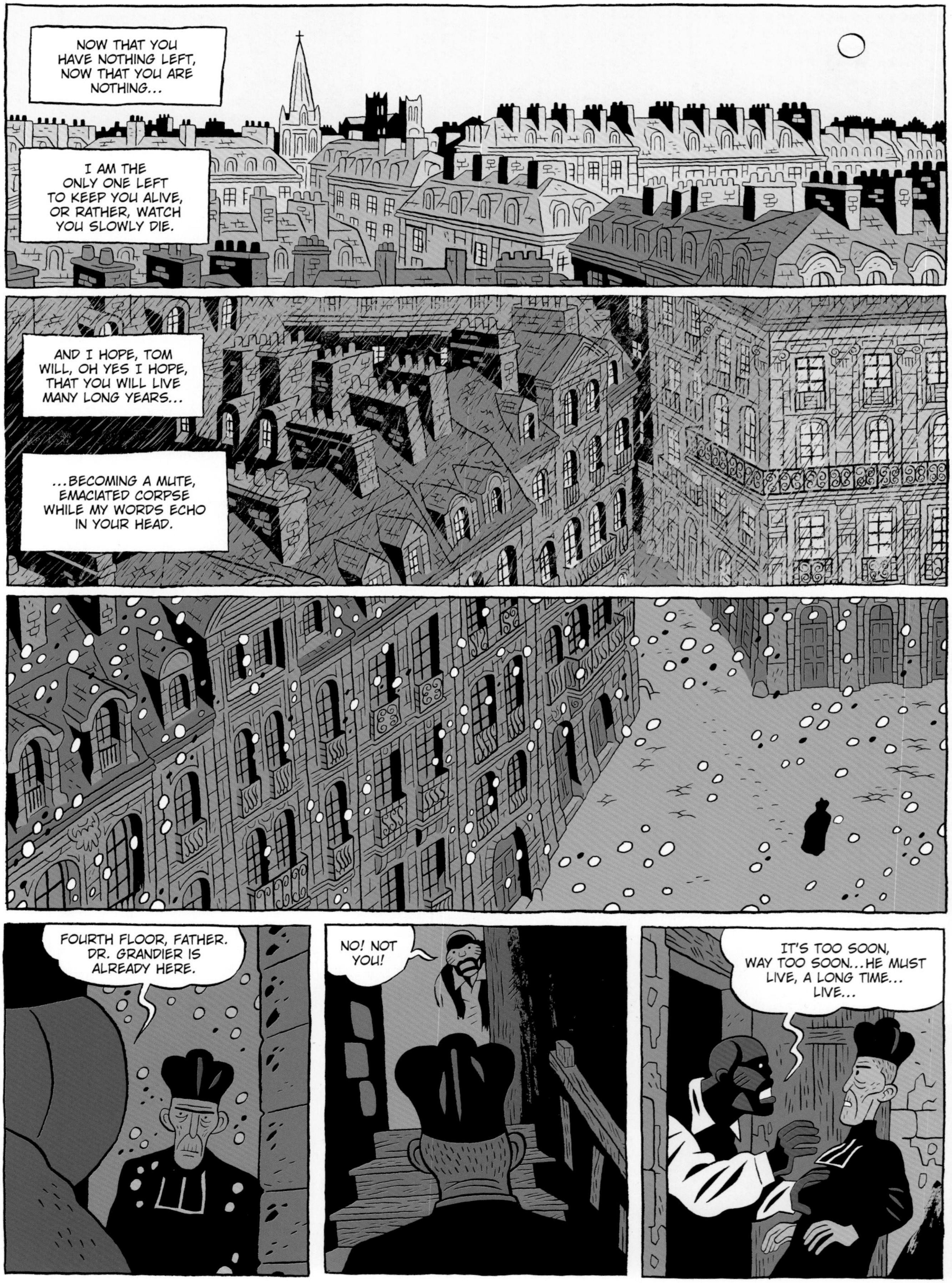
NOW THAT YOU HAVE NOTHING LEFT, NOW THAT YOU ARE NOTHING...
I AM THE ONLY ONE LEFT TO KEEP YOU ALIVE, OR RATHER, WATCH YOU SLOWLY DIE.
AND I HOPE, TOM WILL, OH YES I HOPE, THAT YOU WILL LIVE MANY LONG YEARS...
...BECOMING A MUTE, EMACIATED CORPSE WHILE MY WORDS ECHO IN YOUR HEAD.
FOURTH FLOOR, FATHER. DR. GRANDIER IS ALREADY HERE.
NO! NOT YOU!
IT'S TOO SOON, WAY TOO SOON...HE MUST LIVE, A LONG TIME... LIVE...

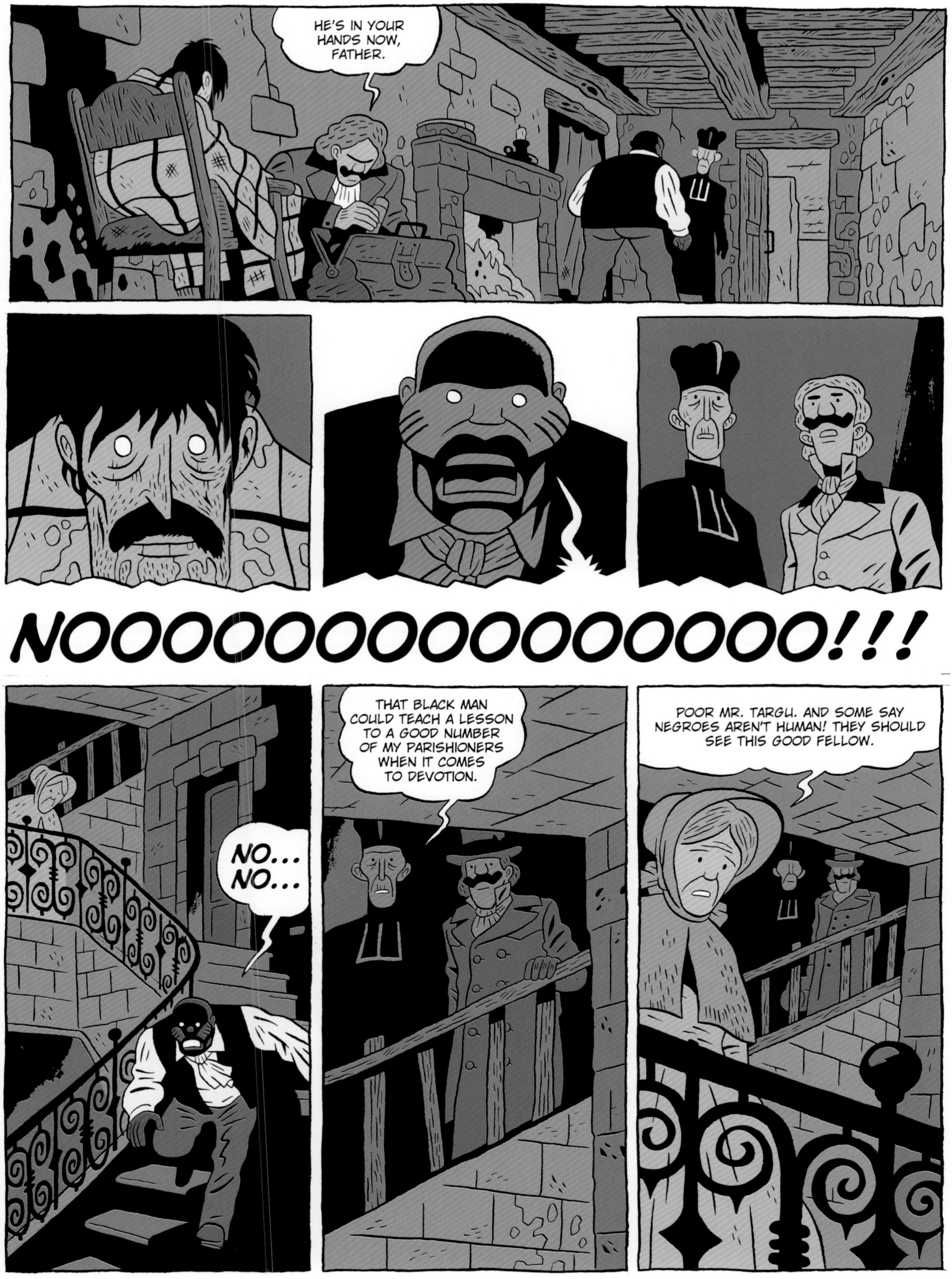
HE'S IN YOUR HANDS NOW, FATHER.
NOOOOOOOOOOOOOOOOO!!!
NO... NO...
THAT BLACK MAN COULD TEACH A LESSON TO A GOOD NUMBER OF MY PARISHIONERS WHEN IT COMES TO DEVOTION.
POOR MR. TARGU. AND SOME SAY NEGROES AREN'T HUMAN! THEY SHOULD SEE THIS GOOD FELLOW.

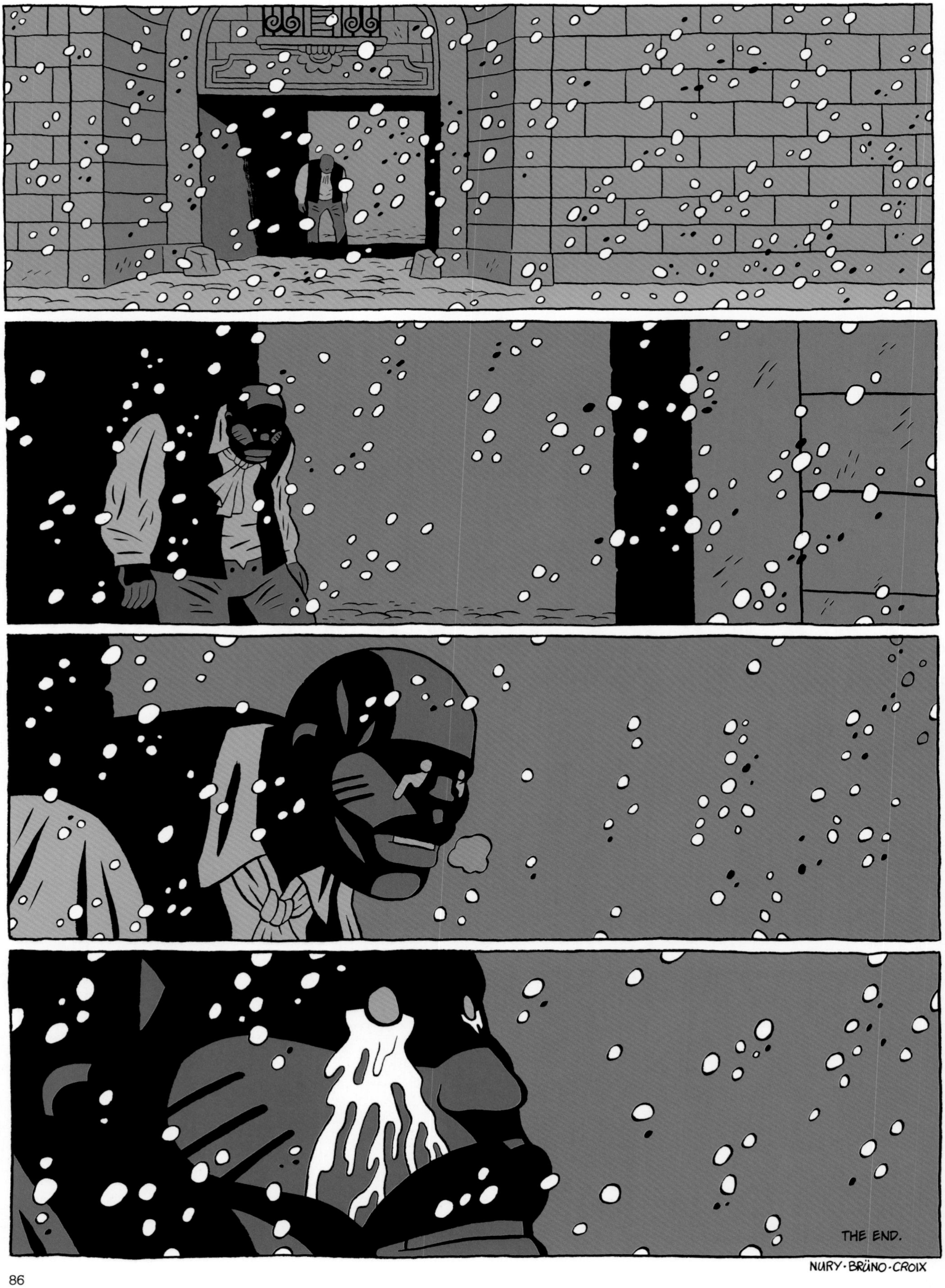
THE END.

NURY · BRÜNO · CROIX

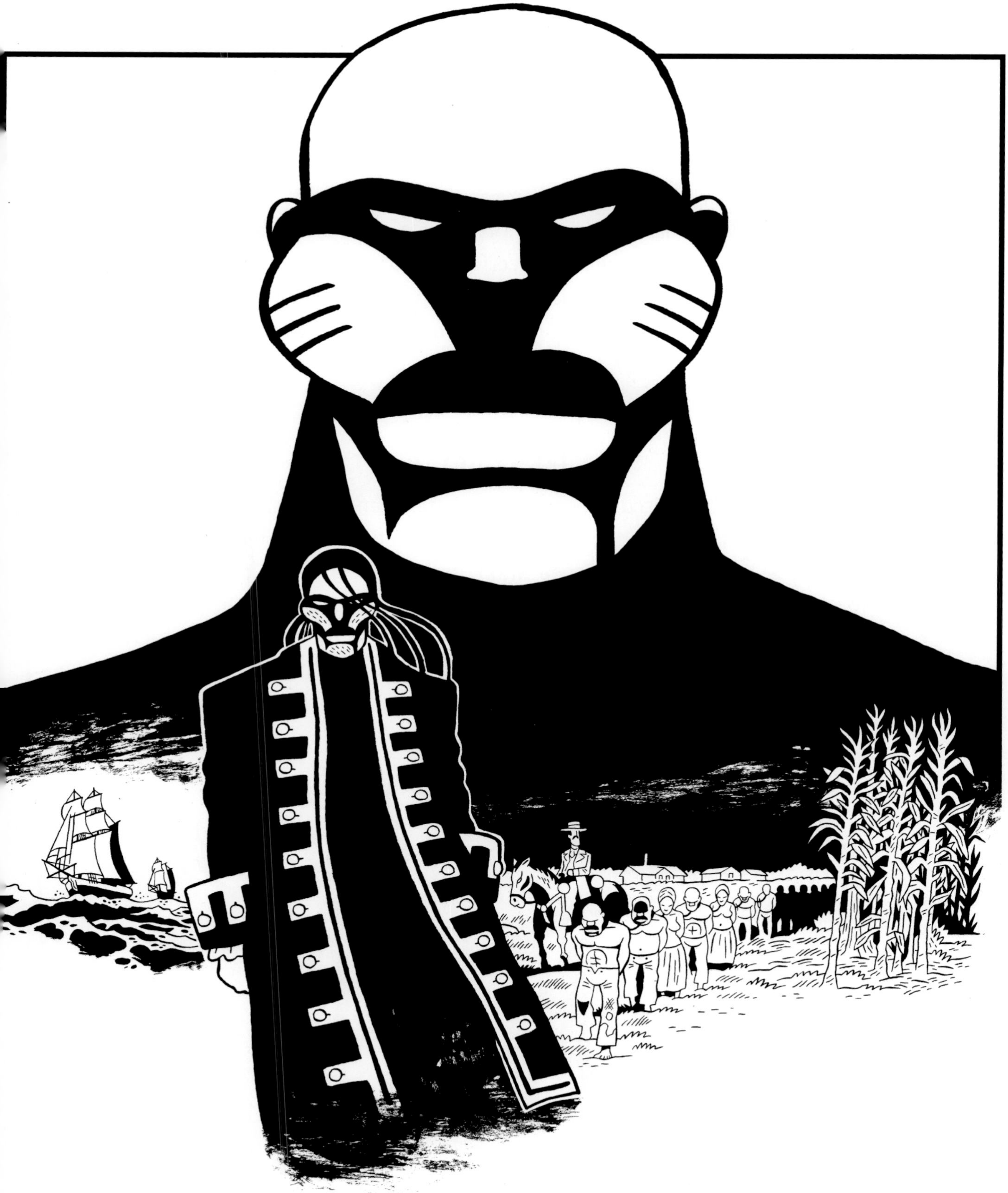

CREATOR BIOS

FABIEN NURY

FABIEN NURY is an award-winning French comics writer, beginning his career in comics by co-writing W.E.S.T with Xavier Dorison. He went on to pen *I Am Legion*, which was translated into eight languages. Another success was *Once Upon a Time in France*, for which he received the 2011 prize for best series at the Angouleme International Comics Festival. He is most recently known for the original graphic novels, *Tyler Cross*, *The Death of Stalin* – which was adapted into a hit movie by writer/director Armando Iannucci in 2017 – and *Death to the Tsar*.

BRÜNO

Brüno was born and raised in Germany, and after spending a year at the Ecole Estienne in Paris, he moved to Rennes, where he obtained a master's degree in Visual Arts. In 2007 he was signed with French publisher Dargaud, where he continues his successful collaborations, notably with Fabien Nury. In 2013, the two authors launched a new series, *Tyler Cross*. Brüno lives and works in Nantes, France.